VENICE

LAB

RETHINKING ST. MARK'S SQUARE

edited by

LUCA MOLINARI

Marsilio Arte

1831

The city of Venice has always held a special place throughout the long history of Assicurazioni Generali. In 1832, a few months after its foundation, the Company opened its first offices in the Procuratie Vecchie, in St. Mark's Square, and since 1848 the winged lion, symbol of the city, has been Generali's internationally recognised logo.

This unique bond, which has grown stronger over the years, recently witnessed the addition of a new chapter that also represents the culmination of Generali's most ambitious project for the renewal of the Marciana area. It began with the reopening of the Royal Gardens at the end of 2019. At the height of the celebrations for the Group's one hundred and ninetieth anniversary and after a major five-year renovation, this iconic building opens its doors to the public for the first time ever, becoming the home of The Human Safety Net and a space devoted to dialogue and the exchange of ideas to overcome the key social challenges in today's world.

At Generali, we believe that companies play a role that goes far beyond their business activity and can make a difference for the countries in which they operate, through actions that would leave a significant and lasting mark on communities. With this in mind, in 2017 we launched The Human Safety Net, a global movement of "people helping people" which aims to develop the potential of those who live in vulnerable conditions for their own benefit and that of their community. Thus, The Human Safety Net's mission, based on enhancing human potential, has much in common with the values that have always defined Venice as a welcoming place for meetings, exchanges and innovation.

The restoration of the Procuratie Vecchie, an extremely complex building in terms of architecture, provided an opportunity to involve a wide range of talented professionals, capable of harmonising local traditions with the most innovative techniques. Moreover, an ongoing and stimulating dialogue has been established with public authorities, with a view to invest in an asset that belongs to the entire community and that brings prestige to the Venice World Capital of Sustainability project. The result of this shared effort is truly extraordinary: a building in one of the most beautiful squares in the world restored to its former glory. This is even more special in light of the challenges posed by the pandemic over the past two years.

We would therefore like to extend our deepest and most heartfelt gratitude to David Chipperfield Architects and all of the other people involved, for having contributed to turning a vision started long ago into a reality that is a symbol of the city of tomorrow. Venice is a unique city, committed to building an inclusive and sustainable future leveraging its unparalleled historic and cultural heritage.

GABRIELE GALATERI DI GENOLA
Chairman Generali Group

PHILIPPE DONNET
Assicurazioni Generali Group CEO

Venice belongs to both Venetians and the whole world. It's a local community and at once a universal icon, and St. Mark's Square, a treasure trove full of wonders, represents its beating heart.

The restoration project, promoted by Assicurazioni Generali to refurbish and regenerate the Procuratie Vecchie building, aims to enhance this relationship between the building, the public space, and local identity, opening it up to citizens and visitors, while assigning it a social function.

The project is part of a wide-ranging discussion on the Marciana area and, more generally, on the future of the lagoon city. Venice, with its stunning beauty and extreme vulnerability, challenges and questions us.

Here, the well-known issues that afflict all Cities of Art combine with the peculiar conditions of a unique and distinctive territory, marked by such a precious and fragile context, thus becoming amplified.

The commitment to preserve this extraordinary amalgam of art, culture, and landscape, to improve this living, dynamic city which is at once a symbolic place recognised all over the world, must be turned into a laboratory of new ideas and good practices, with courage and vision.

In these pages, readers will find many insights and interesting ideas.

DARIO FRANCESCHINI
Minister of Culture

What does the history of a building teach us? What does it tell us about its functions? How can an urban regeneration project fit into a social context that has changed over the centuries?

These are legitimate questions that arise from the vision of Generali, which aims to pinpoint the future social function of the Procuratie Vecchie in St. Mark's Square, Venice; notably, the building will become the headquarters of the Human Safety Net Foundation following a restoration project promoted by the insurance company and completed in 2021, timed to coincide with the one hundred and ninetieth anniversary of its establishment.

There are many links between Generali and Venice, starting with the Winged Lion of Saint Mark, which in 1848 the Group chose as its official logo.

Included in the monumental, architectural, and symbolic complex of St. Mark's Square, the Procuratie Vecchie building was the abode of the Procurators, the powerful magistrates of La Serenissima in charge of various aspects of the life of the Republic of Venice and of supporting citizens in need. This same concern is shared by The Human Safety Net Foundation, whose philanthropic mission is to help suffering people in countries where the Insurance Group is present, with a focus on parenting and disadvantaged children.

After the restoration carried out by architect David Chipperfield, who resorted to avant-garde technology but also to experts in the preservation and restoration of frescoes, the building will be opened to the public, offering exhibition areas related to the activities of the Foundation, an auditorium, and spaces for new and experimental design solutions. As a result, the city will regain one of its unique urban spaces, once again alive, inclusive, and serving as a source of inspiration for the community.

All this represents a fitting conclusion to a project of urban regeneration and social enhancement that also involved the Royal Gardens of Venice, whose restoration was also co-funded by Generali, and that like the Procuratie Vecchie, have been returned to the community preserving their history and identity, while also promoting their modern and sustainable use.

Indeed, in our collective imagination, the Procuratie Vecchie are a recognisable landmark of Venice, a dynamic space that continues to evolve, and somewhat linked to the process undertaken by the city to become the world capital for sustainability: this will allow Venice to stand as an adequate environmental, economic, social, and urban planning model for the future, capable of inspiring increasingly virtuous practices for sustainable lifestyles and growth.

I will not deal in depth with this topic, since the present publication with its wealth of images, essays, and insights by experts and scholars, provides a detailed description of the various stages of the work; rather, I would like to underline how the synergies implemented for this restoration project have been productive, and how collaboration between public institutions and private companies always proves fundamental when collective interests are at stake, as in the case of a building like this one, which is once again made available to the community.

Lastly, I would like to extend my gratitude to Generali for showing sensitivity and commitment towards sustainability, for recognising the value of the Procuratie Vecchie, and being able to grasp this building's true essence, since—in the words of Le Corbusier—"Architecture is a thing of art, a phenomenon of the emotions."

LUCA ZAIA
President of Veneto Region

There is no doubt that St. Mark's Square, the same square that the Polish author Mieczysław Kozłowski defined as the "heart of Venice," is one of the most famous and breathtaking places in the world. No words can truly describe the emotions of those who set foot in the square for the first time. Here it's easy to be captivated by its amazing monumentality, grandeur, magnificence, and beauty. Over the centuries, the square has managed to expand and transform, following the foundation and development of Venice, of which, precisely this year, we are celebrating the sixteen-hundredth anniversary. This place has been the stage for so much of the history and traditions of the city, and today, thanks to the synergy between public institutions and private companies, we are restoring its former glory to pass it on, even more beautiful, to future generations.

Assicurazioni Generali, with its commitment to renew the spaces of the Procuratie Vecchie through an impressive restoration project, actively participates in this virtuous path. These regenerated locations will be given a new perspective, with a special focus on social and cultural innovation; it's no coincidence that these are also the core values of The Human Safety Net, the foundation which will be a permanent presence in this prestigious part of St. Mark's Square. Such a path fully embodies the spirit of a city that throughout its history has always made its tradition the starting point for promoting the development and growth of its community from a cultural, social, economic, and relational point of view.

The city has always grasped the opportunities offered to it and continues to do so. This time, this goal was achieved by partnering with Assicurazioni Generali in this praiseworthy renovation of the Procuratie Vecchie and also, always remaining in the Marciana area, by supporting the restoration of the Royal Gardens, so as to reopen them to the public. These actions are part of a broader project, which involves the safeguarding of three symbolic areas of the city. This, in fact, was also the case for the Rialto Area—a place linked to trade—with the restoration of Ponte di Rialto; this is also being carried out at the Arsenale—the symbolic area of the naval domination of La Serenissima over the seas—through the restoration of the Tese and the promotion of the Boat Show; and also in the Marciana area—a symbolic location of the political-religious power of the Republic—where we are engaged, for instance, in the complete renovation of the Ponte della Zecca and in a set of actions aimed at repairing the damage done by the exceptional high water on November 2019, which will include the consolidation and complete refurbishment of the Royal Gardens embankment, as well as the safeguarding of its historic maritime pines. Not to mention the important investments made for the recovery and refurbishment of the Palazzo Ducale facades and, more recently, the 7.3 million euros made available by the Ministry of Culture for the renovation and preservation of St. Mark's Basilica and the Procuratie Nuove courtyards.

I would therefore once again like to extend my gratitude to the Generali Group, because together we are honouring the Lion of St. Mark, a symbol that we share and represents Venice all around the world; and because together we have ensured that this square, the "heart of the city," will continue to beat, keeping alive the ardour and passion of Venice, which proves, even on this occasion, to be the oldest city of the future.

LUIGI BRUGNARO
Mayor of Venice

GEDA

A square is the place of meeting and coexistence *par excellence*, a truly proxemic space in which people can feel at ease. Here, we see the signs of living together which, through beauty, offer a vision that is at once particular and universal.

St. Mark's Square, with its Cathedral Basilica named after the Evangelist, stands as a unique example of elegance and beauty, having become a symbol of the city as well as its most iconic image all around the world. This universal value must be preserved, above and beyond any individual interest.

Such a human environment—forged by faith, history, art, and identity—is the result of centuries in which every restoration work has made the heart of Venice more alive and vibrant.

In a society that is increasingly a global—and hopefully also supportive—community, cities are called upon to preserve spaces in all walks of life. These values have always been a virtuous feature of Venice acting as driving forces behind the city's growth.

It is critical that, even today, this sensitivity should be an integral part of projects that imply not only the restoration of the most significant urban spaces, but also represent an opportunity to reboot the city's dynamism by combining civil and religious traditions, being mindful of the past, while opening up to a future in which every citizen feels involved.

The restoration of the Procuratie Vecchie—promoted by Assicurazioni Generali—takes the merit for enhancing historic architecture in the centre of Venice.

This impressive project, which is visible to all, also has the merit of hosting The Human Safety Net, a foundation established to support the most fragile communities in the countries where the Generali Group is present.

This investment recalls the history and vocation of Venice, offering a valuable example in the framework of contemporary projects. Nowadays, the city has the task of linking the past and the future, with an eye to the most vulnerable situations.

Hopefully, Assicurazioni Generali's project will pave the way for other institutions to "inhabit" the city, promoting actions capable of making Venice a place of encounter and relationships again—connecting even very "distant" people—as the history of the Serenissima Republic clearly shows.

FRANCESCO MORAGLIA
Patriarch of Venice

RESTORATION WORKS IN A SYMBOLIC PLACE

FROM HISTORY TO GLOBAL IMPACT

AMAZEMENT AND EMOTION

SIMONE BEMPORAD

Seeing the Procuratie Vecchie in St. Mark's Square for the first time in my role at Generali, coming from San Moisè, I realised I was witnessing an unexpressed wonder. In 2014 the Procuratie looked like a soulless architectural masterpiece. Given that its last tenants were wiretapping companies working for the Office of Venice's Public Prosecutor, you can imagine the situation: under nineteenth-century frescoed vaults, we found paper scraps stuck to the wall with tape and pins. Hence, the idea of fully restoring the Procuratie arose from the power of an image, capable of freeing the beauty, neglected over time, of one of the most iconic buildings ever, standing in one of the most visited squares in a city where the whole world feels at home. A heritage that must be shared with all humanity.

This volume tells the story of an idea arising from amazement and emotion. However, the project was highly innovative because we wanted to combine an extraordinary "container" (the Procuratie) with a "content" that would motivate the massive investment. Although restoring beauty needed no justifications, we immediately discussed the issue of not limiting ourselves to doing something that was "merely" beautiful. We also wanted to give meaning to the architectural project, and create a new identity, something that could represent the legacy of Assicurazioni Generali as the advocate for millions of future customers around the world, and a source of pride for thousands—whether they be employees or agents—who carry our banner every day. So, why not go further, why not think outside the box, taking into account customers, employees, and agents, and turn the Procuratie into an open space, making it the hub of a worldwide network to generate an impact thanks to Generali, yet going beyond Generali. We knew from the start: there would be no restoration without a unique, groundbreaking idea. And vice versa: no contribution to the community that Generali was able to provide would have had the strength and skills needed without a powerful symbol.

During the tender, which involved projects by some of the greatest living architects, we visited the David Chipperfield Architects studio in Milan towards the end of 2016. Unlike other competitors, David asked us to show his project in his offices in Milan, instead of taking it to Generali's headquarters, at that time in Piazza Cordusio. Upon entering the palatial office, with drawings, photographs, and sketches hanging everywhere, as well as 3D models on a number of tables, I asked Giuseppe Zampieri and Cristiano Billia in which area of the studio the projects related to the Procuratie were.

"Everything you see here is about your project!" answered the architects, to whose genius we owe the idea of a restoration project that today leaves everyone breathless. Sketches of the Procuratie were everywhere, wherever we looked. These architects' all-encompassing passion would later create connections between the Chipperfield studio and businesses, local artisans, designers, institutions, Generali's employees, citizens, associations, artists, photographers, writers, and researchers. Their passion brought people together.

Indeed, Venice belongs to those who photograph it, like Guido Guidi, who captured the raw beauty of this ancient, giant building that has been renewed from within, in a surprising way, by breathing new life into it. In his photos, one can find hard-working people as well as the promise of what the structure, step by step, would become; or Diana Bagnoli, who captured on film the faces, effort, ingenuity, and dedication of all those who worked on this project.

Venice belongs to those who design new urban spaces, secret gardens, places for meeting and contemplation, such as Paolo Pejrone, Itai Palti, and Ico Migliore. Venice belongs to those who study it, like Andrew Hopkins, Michel Lussault, and Simon Anholt. It belongs to those who value its historical heritage, like Emanuela Carpani, and to those who, like Alberto Torsello, have chosen to devote their work to protecting and preserving its beauty.

The city belongs to those who live there, to those who visit it as tourists, and to those who want to leave a mark, such as Adele Re Rebaudengo, Renata Codello, and Orna Cohen. Venice inspires those who tell stories about it, as Alberto Toso Fei and Arthur Brooks do, and those who make it a symbol of human condition, like Guadalupe Nettel; those who animate it and emphasise its dynamic nature, like Davide Rampello and Cesare Benelli. Venice belongs to all of us, who believed in this new challenge, and to all of you, who are holding this book.

Like the essays in this volume, the meaning given to the Procuratie is also the result of a shared responsibility, the one we have as companies, as citizens, as individuals, as human beings, not to remain indifferent to the imbalances of society, not to avoid the opportunity to personally contribute and be a part of a positive change.

There are many areas that require collective efforts, and Generali has made choices, contributing with its skills and its global network in any domain where it can help build a fairer and more inclusive future. This goal is supported by The Human Safety Net programmes, which focus on developing human potential in the most disadvantaged contexts, whether they be families in need, to ensure that their children, during their first, decisive six years, will not suffer life-long traumas; or refugees who can set up their own business and become entrepreneurs in the host countries: none are irrelevant to social prosperity.

Centuries ago, the Venetian Procurators oversaw issues concerning the community. Today the Procuratie are returning to their old purpose: the building, in addition to hosting the headquarters of The Human Safety Net Foundation, will promote activities—whether they deal with art or a better future, such as the newly established Foundation for Venice as the World Capital of Sustainability, strongly supported by Philippe Donnet—capable of interpreting this desire to make the container and the content a unique, original, and long-lasting project.

The spirit of the Procuratie shines through in its details, materials, and architectural solutions, resulting from a project that does not mandate, but rather aims to inherit and complete the pre-existing, antique structures. The Procuratie's design expresses a vision on how to work and interact in the twenty-first century, in which tradition and future can merge.

Is it a finished project? Can we truly say that it is complete and immutable? The destiny of Venice, as that of the Procuratie and St. Mark's Square, is not only linked to conservation, but also to the ability to innovate, to envisage some new leaps forward from time to time, bridging the past and the future; like two banks of a canal, they must be linked to carry visitors forward, towards another stage of their journey. So it is that the Procuratie project represents both a praise of the past and a suggestion for the future; it's a space that can connect even more with the square around it and open towards the sky, to let new light filter into its rooms.

PIAZZA SAN MARCO

– RESTORATION WORKS IN A SYMBOLIC PLACE –

A LIVING BODY: ST. MARK'S SQUARE AND ITS ARCHITECTURE

ANDREW HOPKINS

For most of its history, St. Mark's Square could not be seen from the air. Before the advent of the jet age, the best one could do to admire the finest drawing-room in Europe—as Napoleon Bonaparte (1769–1821) supposedly called it—from an elevated position, was to climb up the Campanile, the bell tower that with its thousand-year-old bronze bells was rebuilt where it was and as it was, after its collapse on 14 July 1902, despite voices calling for a contemporary building to replace it. There, from above, through the white Istrian stone loggias with four arched openings on each side that had been added after an earthquake in 1512 had damaged it, one could survey the most celebrated square in the world, a masterwork of architecture and urbanism.

Yet, St. Mark's Square, like the former ducal chapel from which it takes its name, has never been static and is best understood as a living organism because, even today, a celebrated contemporary architect, David Chipperfield (b. 1953), has just completed the transformation of a series of spaces in the Procuratie Vecchie. This latest contribution to the life of the square, almost a quarter of the way through the twenty-first century, will surely not be the last, and each century and its architects have made interventions and incursions both superb, controversial and divisive. Travelling backwards, contribution by contribution, heading towards the misty and uncertain beginnings of the piazza, allows us to bring into focus each change, while avoiding the trap of a search for its origins, as remote and difficult to trace as those of Venice itself.

As symbolic heart and soul of La Serenissima, the piazza—in fact composed of three parts, the main piazza, the piazzetta between Palazzo Ducale and the Libreria, and the Piazzetta dei Leoncini on the south side of St. Mark's—has maintained its magnetism long after the doges disappeared for good in 1797. As recently as 1997, two hundred years after Napoleon invaded and brought the Republic to an end, the assault on the Campanile of 8–9 May 1997 was staged by the secessionist commando the *Serenissimi*, whose *Tanko*—a truck disguised as a tank—occupied the square. Much more damaging to the preservation of the piazza's unique cultural patrimony was the disastrous Pink Floyd concert held in the *bacino* (the San Marco Basin) in 1989. The astonishing photograph taken at the time by Graziano Arici (b. 1949) captures once and for all just how potentially damaging mass gatherings, as well as mass tourism, can be to architectural heritage: to enjoy the concert, several "privileged" but impertinent spectators even perched themselves atop the capitals and columns of the (rebuilt) Loggetta by Jacopo Sansovino (1486–1570).

The piazza was also "invaded" by James Bond in the 1979 film *Moonraker* where 007 escapes his enemies by flicking the switch, thereby transforming his motorised gondola into a hybrid hovercraft. These three human assaults on the piazza in modern times are a world away from the more genteel visitors of the past who flocked there, to have their picture

St. Mark's Square during the Pink Floyd concert, July 1989.

As symbolic heart and soul of La Serenissima, the piazza has maintained its magnetism long after the doges disappeared for good in 1797.

taken. But these examples are nothing compared to the *acqua alta* of almost two metres that assaulted Venice and St. Mark's Square on 3 November 1966, when gondolas were able to sail into and around the square. Untold water damage was done to the buildings surrounding the piazza and the only positive outcome, consequently, was the founding of various groups dedicated to preserving the cultural heritage of the city, including Save Venice and Venice in Peril.

Around a decade earlier, in 1957, Carlo Scarpa (1906–1978), the most important Venetian architect of the twentieth century, was commissioned by Adriano Olivetti (1901–1960), of the avant-garde family of typewriter designers, to create a showroom to display the firm's products in a shop under the portico of the Procuratie Vecchie. Situated on the corner of the Sotoportego del Cavalletto, a mezzanine gallery half the size of the ground floor is reached by a syncopated series of horizontal slabs of this spectacular staircase, which also displays a calculator at the beginning of the ascent; machines in various colours are displayed in the window fronting the sotoportego. Scarpa chose the primary colours red, yellow and blue, plus white, for the ground floor marble flooring and Murano glass. Large picture windows bring together and connect the interior and exterior spaces, so that the interior's set-piece fountain, in which water flows into a rectangular basin of smooth black marble, with its striking and perfectly perched copper sculpture by Alberto Viani (1906–1999), is easily visible from the piazza. In the mezzanine above there is a shift in materials with the introduction of much teak wood, including hinged shelves for displaying the products. An ingeniously camouflaged side door is to be found beside the large external Olivetti logo set on a rough stone slab. The extensive tempering with other, more traditional materials and colours, enabled Scarpa to

The interior of Carlo Scarpa's Olivetti showroom, 1957.

Scarpa chose the primary colours red, yellow and blue, plus white, for the ground floor marble flooring and Murano glass.

introduce concrete into the piazza and, as has been noted, these other materials were used to warm too stark a modernity. For the first time in Venice, it became possible for concrete to be opulent.

A century before, in 1858, the earliest and most famous café in the world, Caffè Florian, occupying the ground floor of part of the Procuratie Nuove, was entirely renovated by the Venetian architect Ludovico Cadorin (1824–1892) with interior decorations that survive today. Founded in 1720 by Floriano Francesconi with the name *Alla Venezia Trionfante* (To Venice Triumphant), Venetians in their dialect spoke of "going to Florian's" ("*andémo da Floriàn*"), hence the founder's nephew's decision to change its name in 1797, after Napoleon's invasion. The first three decades of the establishment had been so successful, given the frequency with which Venetian nobles visited it that, in 1750, the Oriental Room and the Room of the Senate were added to the original Chinese Room and Entrance. Even today, early in the morning waiters prepare for the long day that awaits them, with the arrival of the orchestra and the onslaught of tourists.

One of Napoleon's most symbolically brutal acts when annexing Venice, was to order the demolition of the small church of San Geminiano in 1807, in order to build, at the other end of the piazza opposite St. Mark's, an imperial staircase leading to a sumptuous ballroom enjoying a spectacular view onto the piazza and the cafés Quadri and Florian. The pioneering bird's-eye view map of Venice of 1500 by Jacopo de'

Jacopo De' Barbari, *Perspective View of Venice*, 1500, detail. Museo Correr, Venice.

Barbari (ca. 1460/70–before 1516), a detailed woodcut print made up of six sheets, accurately depicts San Geminiano's position at the western end of the piazza seen from the side and from a distance. This was the church's second location, because the earlier Veneto-Byzantine version, situated on land which is now the centre of the piazza, had been demolished by Doge Sebastiano Ziani (d. 1178) in a series of enlargements to the square undertaken by him and, later, his son Doge Pietro Ziani (d. 1230). That first "creative" destruction was perceived as insulting and ignominious by the pope, despite the fact the Venetian church was subject to *ius patronatus*, which meant it was under the direct patronage of the doge, rather than of the Holy See. As a consequence, an apologetic annual visit was paid by the doge and his government to the church, which had been reconstructed in the mid-twelfth century at the end of the piazza and then again rebuilt starting in 1505 by Cristoforo da Legname and completed by Sansovino in the 1550s with an Istrian stone facade. Napoleon's symbolic and presumptuous demolition, to replace it with the Ala Napoleonica (the Napoleonic Wing), a relatively repetitive and monotonous composition that annihilated the asymmetry of the church's location, between the extended Procuratie Vecchie and the Procuratie Nuove, is indicative of a tendency in neoclassical design principles that is hard to admire.

In the seventeenth century, the construction of the Procuratie Nuove was completed by Baldassare Longhena (1598–1682) in a simplified composition compared to that with which Vincenzo Scamozzi (1548–1616) had commenced. Scamozzi's sumptuous inner courtyard, with its Doric, Ionic and Corinthian columns together with elegantly framed windows, reveals his intention to match the extraordinarily sculptural exterior looking over the square. Where these luxurious residences set above the ground level arcades and shops joined Sansovino's Libreria, in line with the bell tower, one can observe clearly the difference in the heights and proportions of the classical orders in Sansovino's earlier two-storey composition and Scamozzi's later three-storey construction.

Sansovino's Libreria was just one of a trio of buildings designed by the architect in the 1530s for Andrea Gritti (1484–1538), doge from 1523 and his Procurators. The side where the Libreria is now had long been considered unsuitable because of the presence of prostitutes and food shops on the corner between Sansovino's 1536 Zecca or Mint and the 1538 Loggetta for Venetian nobles. The state of their construction is shown in the spectacular print by Jost Amman (1539–1591) of around 1565, depicting the procession on Ascension Day of the doge to the Bucintoro, the ceremonial state barge. The Zecca, in its original two-storey configuration is shown as complete (the third storey was added later in the century), as is the Loggetta at the base of the bell tower built of fine coloured marbles and adorned with bronze statues and bas-reliefs depicting allegorical themes to do with the origins of the city. Completion of Sansovino's sixteen-bay Libreria was impeded by

Continuous efforts were made over the centuries to improve and embellish the piazza on which civic, ecclesiastical and confraternal ceremonies took place.

the house of ill-repute in front of it, where courtesans or *cortegiane* advertised themselves from the first-floor windows. This sorry state of affairs was only remedied towards the end of the sixteenth century.

The Loggetta had then to be completely rebuilt using original fragments and new technologies in 1902 after the spectacular collapse of the bell tower.

Amman's view records one of the many annual processions, known as *andate ducali*, that animated the piazza throughout the year. Because these events represented the Republic of Venice and its head of state, the doge—whose office was defined as *primus inter pares,* first among equals—, continuous efforts were made over the centuries to improve and embellish the piazza on which civic, ecclesiastical and confraternal ceremonies took place. The procession Amman depicts snakes between the two ancient columns, the official and symbolic entrance to the city topped with statues of the patron saints of Venice, Saint Todaro and the Lion of Saint Mark. To the right is Palazzo Ducale, the doge's palace, the prime Gothic monument with its "upside-down" arrangement of two open loggias supporting the solid walls of the third storey (which contains the Maggior Consiglio meeting room) revetted with Istrian stone and red Verona marble in a diaper pattern that resembles an Impressionist painting: no surprise that Claude Monet (1840–1926) painted several versions of this iconic building and its reflection in the dappled waters of the *bacino*.

Amman's print represents the ducal chapel, St. Mark's, custodian of the body of Saint Mark the

The Napoleonic Wing.

Evangelist (5–68 CE) which was brought here from Alexandria in Egypt. The church was enlarged and rebuilt several times and the structure seen by visitors today dates largely from the second half of the eleventh century. Its appearance was, however, radically altered following the Fourth Crusade, undertaken at the beginning of the thirteenth century when numerous spoils from Constantinople were deployed to adorn both the interior and exterior of the building, covering up most of the original brick structure set below the five domes of the quincunx.

How the exterior of St. Mark's looked in 1500 is accurately recorded in de' Barbari's view. It also depicts a very recent, relatively diminutive but highly symbolic addition to the piazza: the splendid Torre dell'Orologio designed by Mauro Codussi (1440–1504) dated around 1497. The two bays either side are slightly later additions and it is the taller central bay that is of most importance, not only because at ground level is the arched entranceway to the Merceria, the street that leads all the way to the Rialto market and bridge, but also because the four central storeys, concluding with the white stone figure of the Lion of Saint Mark and topped by the mechanical bronze bell-strikers, correspond to the series of diminishing proportions in height mentioned by Leon Battista Alberti (1404–1472) in his architectural treatise published in 1480. Given this display of architectural erudition, it is not surprising to learn that a few years later the construction was enhanced by three bronze flagstaves commissioned by Doge Leonardo Loredan (1436–1511).The doge broke a long-standing convention by having his profile portrait placed on them, scenographically framing the Torre dell'Orologio viewed from the piazzetta. These bases with their flagpoles and flags fluttering in the breeze are a demonstration of the effective creation of a perspectival view in an urban setting.

The completion of the Libreria at its end, towards the waters of the *bacino,* conferred some kind of completion to the piazzetta looking out to the islands of San Giorgio Maggiore and Giudecca. And also the view of the ceremonial entrance to Venice, as it was seen from the island of San Giorgio, was completed, so to speak, by 1600 with the addition of the New Prisons, right of Palazzo Ducale, and of what will become known as the Ponte dei Sospiri, the Bridge of Sighs connecting the two buildings. West of Sansovino's Zecca the old granaries used to close the scenographic backdrop of the sweeping and panoramic view from afar. During the first Napoleonic period the granaries were demolished to make way for the Giardini Reali, the Royal Gardens of Venice.

Returning to the viewpoint from which this brief account began, but now at ground level, the most important view of the piazza, dating from 1496 by Gentile Bellini (ca. 1429–1507), is an enormous canvas that captures the ceremonial life of the piazza at the

Jost Amman, *Procession of the Doge towards the Bucintoro on Ascension Day*, about 1565, detail.

end of the fifteenth century. The feast of *Corpus Domini* was one of the most important processional celebrations held in the piazza annually and this oil painting was commissioned by the ancient confraternity of the Scuola Grande di San Giovanni Evangelista. To the left are the Procuratie Vecchie before the addition of the Torre dell'Orologio a year or two later, while to the right is the Campanile and its contiguous buildings, forty years before Sansovino exceptionally decided to separate the Campanile and make it independent, significantly pushing back the alignment of what were to become the Procuratie Nuove towards the *bacino*, also opening up the view from San Geminiano on the right hand side and making the piazza much more spacious and open to the sky. The procession comes out of the Porta della Carta, the ceremonial axis leading from the interior of Palazzo Ducale and out towards the Loggetta, and hence snaking around the piazza, at this time and for centuries paved with red clay bricks, unlike the glum unfriendly grey slabs that replaced them in the early eighteenth century.

Bellini's painting also depicts in all their splendour the celebrated Quadriga, the four ancient gilded bronze horses, stolen from Constantinople during the Fourth Crusade, and deposited on the facade of St. Mark's, before they suffered a series of ignominious removals, first by Napoleon who had them transported to Paris, and then during World War I, and again in 1977 when they were removed for restoration, toured around the world and returned to Venice to become part of the inexorable move towards placing originals in museums to protect them from the disastrous atmospheric and climatic conditions of the world outside in the twentieth and twenty-first centuries.

For the first time in centuries, 2020 and 2021 have seen the piazza empty of the usual flock of tourists over-running it. An at once sad and inspiring sight, that architectural historians, architects, photographers, and cultivated tourists have been able to appreciate without the usual cacophony of visitors. So too, in these strange times, David Chipperfield, without being seen, has been transforming some interior spaces of the Procuratie Vecchie, now revealed to the public and in this splendid publication. Yet another brilliant contribution to the life of the piazza.

Gentile Bellini, *Procession in St. Mark's Square*, 1496. Gallerie dell'Accademia, Venice.

THE ANCIENT HEART OF VENICE BEATS AGAIN

ALBERTO TOSO FEI

Among the many images captured in Venice by the great masters of photography there is one of 1958 by Pepi Merisio, a snapshot of everyday life in St. Mark's Square. In the foreground there are two girls playing hopscotch: one is jumping and the other, with her hand on her hip, is looking at her. This is their playground; it is normal for them to meet here to play. All around, there are people walking unhurriedly. The square is crowded, but it is not an audience for big occasions; the people do not even look like tourists, which in any case were few in those years: it is probably Sunday, and it is also winter, judging by the clothing, and Venetians are simply experiencing the most important urban space in the city with the normality that is due to them. After all, this is the square that has always been the centre and heart of life in Venice. In the background we see the Procuratie Vecchie, part of the city's everyday landscape since the Middle Ages.

One needs only to go back in time to find other "snapshots" of daily life from other ages, from Canaletto to Longhi, from Guardi to Bellotto, all the way to the nineteenth century, to see how St. Mark's Square has always played a central role in the city's life, and has been the heart of the future of Venice's recent history; a sort of bellwether for the transformation processes which—especially during the twentieth century—have led to a loss of perception of this square as being the focal point of everything, in favour of a museification that has proved to be directly proportional to depopulation.

Generali has been part of this very long evolution as one of the city's main actors until it moved away from Venice. But in the end, like the beautiful circular refraction of waves that swell but that sooner or later recede and return, this institution has returned to make the heart of its square beat once again from the Procuratie, the oldest building of the piazza, the first to mark a stable boundary for the eyes back in twelfth century.

These are the Procuratie Vecchie that we see in a painting by Gentile Bellini, *The Procession in St. Mark's Square*, and which will remain *vecchie* (old) even after their sixteenth-century reconstruction, which however was prior to that of the neighbouring sister building, destined to be known forever as *nuove* (new). Guglielmo dei Grigi and Bartolomeo Bon il Giovane took care of their reconstruction in 1517 after a fire, although their design is sometimes attributed to Mauro Codussi or Scarpagnino. It may have been Jacopo Sansovino who made a final contribution in 1538.

For centuries, from the Procuratie's one hundred windows supported by fifty arches, the procurators of St. Mark—the most prestigious lifelong office in the Republic of Venice, second only to the figure of the doge, appointed by the Great Council for merits acquired during their careers in state administration—overlooked the city. They were entrusted with the care of St. Mark's Basilica, with the protection of the city, of the orphans and of the weak, and administered the execution of wills.

The Procuratie Vecchie housed residences and offices of the *de citra* procurators (*de citra* literally

On the previous page
Pepi Merisio, *In St. Mark's Square*, Venice, 1958.

Canaletto, *St. Mark's Square*, 1723–1724.
Museo Nacional Thyssen-Bornemisza, Madrid.

meaning "on this side" of the Grand Canal), who were in charge of administering the sestieri of St. Mark, Castello and Cannaregio. The other three *de ultra* ("on the other side") sestieri, were instead administered by the provveditori who oversaw that part of the city, reserving finally to the *de supra* (upper) provveditori, the affairs relating to the administration of St. Mark's Basilica, and the Doge's chapel. For many of them, the *procuratoria* was a step towards becoming doge.

So far we have talked about the history, which in Venice always pleasingly blends with legend, to the point of becoming something unique and integral to its very stones and most famous symbols. This is the case of *Pax Tibi Marce Evangelista Meus*, the wording on the city's banner, which echoes the words with which the Archangel Gabriel prophesied to the evangelist the return of his body to the Venetian islands after his death; or that of the legendary birth of Venice itself, on 25 March 421, a date so deeply rooted in Venetian identity that the city adopted a different calendar than the rest of Europe. In a city like this, even riots can turn into something remarkable and unexpected and be quelled through one of the windows of the Procuratie Vecchie.

One late spring of just over seven hundred years ago, the city witnessed a memorable, unprecedented event in the entire history of La Serenissima, and the focal point of this event was the balcony that from the top of the Sotoportego del Cappello overlooks the Merceria dell'Orologio (which at the time had not yet been built).

On 15 June 1310, Bajamonte Tiepolo, together with two other nobles, Marco Querini and Badoero Badoer, launched a conspiracy against the Doge Pietro Gradenigo. The plan was for the rebels to meet at night at Rialto and march at dawn on St. Mark's Square with two groups, one led by Querini arriving from Calle dei Fabbri and the other led by Tiepolo along the Mercerie. Together with Badoer's forces coming from the lagoon they intended to attack Palazzo Ducale. However, Gradenigo was alerted and that same night he summoned his advisers and the representatives of the most prominent families on whose support he could count; he mobilised

Leandro Bassano, *Portrait of Giovanni Francesco Sagredo, Procurator of Saint Mark*, late sixteenth century. Ashmolean Museum, Oxford.

Gabriel Bella, *The Conspiracy of Bajamonte Tiepolo*, eighteenth century. Museo della Fondazione Querini Stampalia, Venice.

the Arsenale and ordered the mayor of Chioggia to intercept Badoer's forces.

The rebels were unable to synchronise their attacks: Tiepolo's group wasted time looting the Rialto Public Treasury and destroying the bridge (which at the time was made of wood), and Badoer did not leave in time due to a strong storm. Querini's group was the first to arrive in St. Mark's Square and immediately engaged in combat during which Querini himself was killed. Tiepolo's men were then attacked in the narrow space of the Mercerie before even reaching the square.

At the height of these violent disorders, a woman, Giustina Rossi, looking out of her window to see what was going on, accidentally dropped a mortar she kept on her balcony on the head of the standard bearer standing next to Bajamonte Tiepolo. The banner fell to the ground and the rebels, devoid of any reference, fled. The Doge's victory was complete: Marco Querini was dead; Badoero Badoer was captured and immediately executed; Tiepolo and the other nobles who had fled to their palaces, were exiled.

To commemorate this event, a marble relief of the old lady of the mortar (*la vecchia del morter*) was placed above the arch, and a stone with the date that is still visible today, was set in the floor. As for Giustina Rossi, the woman whose mortar had knocked down Tiepolo's standard-bearer, she received the reward she asked for: permission to display St. Mark's flag at her window on public holidays, and assurance that the procurators of St. Mark, who owned her house, would never raise the rent. The procurators actually did increase it in 1436, while a great-grandson of the woman was serving in the fleet. In 1468 the man asked and obtained the reinstatement of the old rental fee.

A corollary to this story is a toponymic trace, in the Sotoportego dei Dai which runs under the Procuratie Vecchie leading to a bridge by the same name. Although this sotoportego may owe its name to the Dadi family, legend has it its denomination derives from the events of 15 June 1310, when the conspirators were being chased by the defenders who were encouraged by the people living there who shouted "dai, dai!" (come on, come on!), inviting them to hit the fugitives.

But the Procuratie are also a place where new habits came about, starting a trend that spread

At the height of these violent disorders, a woman, Giustina Rossi, looking out of her window to see what was going on, accidentally dropped a mortar she kept on her balcony on the head of the standard bearer standing next to Bajamonte Tiepolo. The banner fell to the ground and the rebels, devoid of any reference, fled.

throughout the city and well beyond its borders: in 1683 the first shop selling coffee—a *bottega*—was opened under the arches of the Procuratie (in the early seventeenth century coffee was only sold for its medicinal qualities). It's name was *Dell'Arabo* since the business was run by an Arab. Soon there were about thirty coffee places in St. Mark's Square alone, including Quadri and Lavena—both still under the Procuratie Vecchie—and Florian on the opposite side, founded in 1720 as "Triumphant Venice," the world's oldest café, still in business.

Venetian cafés, which in ancient times were called *botteghe da acque* (water shops), throughout the centuries have been meeting places, literary venues (for example, Gasparo Gozzi's newspaper *Gazzetta Veneta* was sold there), but also places where prostitution, espionage, patriotic conspiracy would happened. This was the case in 1848, for instance. The first Italian to mention coffee in the West was a Venetian, Gianfrancesco Morosini, a bailiff in Constantinople, who in his *Relazione della Porta Ottomana*, which he read in 1585 to the Senate, reported how the Turks "not only men of the lower classes, but even those of the upper classes, were in the habit of drinking—publicly, as well as in shops, and in the streets—a black water, as hot as they could take it, which is extracted from a seed and that they call *kahvé*, which they claim has the virtue of keeping a man awake."

It did not take long for coffee to go from being sipped in "the drawing room of the world" to being served in real drawing rooms. One of these salons, which was destined to become a literary and cultural venue, especially between the end of the eighteenth and the nineteenth centuries, was inside the Procuratie Vecchie: a salon that was frequented by personalities such as Ugo Foscolo, Antonio Canova, Madame de Staël, Lord Byron, and Daniele Manin. The person to host these meetings was a very special tenant of the Procuratie: Giustina Renier Michiel, who was a key figure in the final phase of the Republic and who in the early nineteenth century stood as an outspoken and courageous advocate of Venice.

In her youth she was known as the *dosetta*, the *dogarina*. Born into an important family of the Venetian aristocracy, the last two doges, Paolo Renier and Ludovico Manin, were respectively her paternal grandfather and maternal uncle. It was with the first of the two that Giustina Renier Michiel, aged twenty-five, earned her nickname, when she started to replace on official events her grandfather's unpresentable second wife, Margarita Dalmaz (a very young former dancer and tightrope walker the Doge had married in Constantinople), who was too much even for the laid-back late-eighteenth-century Venetian high society.

As a woman of vast culture and great spirit, thanks to her high birth and determination, Giustina Renier Michiel became the historical memory of La Serenissima after its fall and was the proudest defender of the Republic and its institutions: "First and foremost, I am *venezianissima*," she wrote in a letter from 1808. In 1817 she began to have the first issues of her most significant work *Origine delle feste veneziane* (Origins of Venetian Festivities) published in Italian and French, which she compiled during twenty years of research drawing on her personal experience.

She was fluent in French and to refine her English she was the first in Italy to translate some of Shakespeare's works: *Othello*, *Macbeth*, and *Coriolanus*.

Even Napoleon Bonaparte himself regrettably witnessed her great love for the city during the critical

Giustina Rossi, the woman whose mortar had knocked down Tiepolo's standard-bearer, received the reward she asked for: permission to display St. Mark's flag at her window on public holidays, and assurance that the procurators of St. Mark, who owned her house, would never raise the rent.

time of his occupation: "What are you famous for, madam?", the emperor asked her publicly, meeting her in St. Mark's Square in 1807. "For friendship," she replied, obviously in French, without adding anything more. Napoleon pressed on: "And what have you written?" "I've translated some tragedies." "Racine, I guess." "Pardon, Majesty, I translate from English," she replied showing her complete lack of complacency. Bonaparte, annoyed, took leave without a word. But news about that conversation, which had taken place in public, spread across the city, strengthening her image of a courageous and indomitable woman, not afraid to express her feelings and ideas.

Born in Venice, Giustina Renier Michiel lived through two French dominations and the rule of the Habsburg Empire; Venice, which she defined "a magnificent city, which rises above nature"—was also where she died, in her Procuratie Vecchie apartment on 6 April 1832. A few weeks later, Generali would rent some rooms in that same building from the Counts Leonardo and Pietro Gradenigo.

The promoter of this initiative and first director of the Venetian branch of the Assicurazioni Generali Austro-Italiche, which had been founded in Trieste only a few months earlier on 26 December 1831, was Samuele Della Vida from Ferrara, who had already been active in the Venetian Lagoon with his trading firm since 1815. He was to remain in the Generali management until 1875, and from that moment onwards the history of the company began to merge with that of the city; the people working for Generali, the most important Venetian events, and even its symbols became indissolubly linked, starting from that ancient heart.

But let's proceed with order. When Generali opened its branch in Venice the city was under the Hapsburg rule. And the situation was anything but calm: Silvio Pellico had already served ten years of forced labour, first in Venice and then at Spielberg; the young Bandiera brothers were stirring up anti-Austrian sentiments that would lead to their execution during the riots of 1848. The democratic and social tensions emerging in many European states and the independence movements that shook the empire were to lead to revolutionary mass uprisings.

Venice lived 1848 with unparalleled intensity: seventeen months of siege during which the city sustained heavy bombing, cholera and the first aerial bombardment in history, carried out with air balloons. St. Mark's Square obviously witnessed the first stages of the rebellion, with Daniele Manin and Niccolò Tommaseo who, after being released by popular acclaim from the jail in which they were imprisoned for their political activity, were taken to the area between the Basilica and the Procuratie; Manin delivered his speech proclaiming the Venetian Republic standing on a Caffè Florian table.

Who knows if there were members of the Generali management looking at what was happening from their office windows? What we know for certain is that some prominent members of Generali held important roles in the newly formed Republic, while the board of directors decided to remove the adjective "Austro-Italiche" from its heading. So it was during that season of struggles for freedom, that the Assicurazioni Generali came into being.

The three men of the company who covered important institutional roles in the Venetian Republic were two Venetians—Leone Pincherle and Isacco Pesaro Maurogonato—who respectively became Ministers of Commerce and Finance, and Daniele Francesconi from Cordignano, who became head of the Legione Trevigiana. These men appear among the members of the city assembly in the famous painting *Venice will resist the Austrian at all costs, 2 April 1849* by Giovanni Battista Dalla Libera, now at Museo Correr. After the capitulation of the city, in August 1849, they were exiled (Pincherle in Turin and Paris, Maurogonato on the island of Corfu and Francesconi who was also imprisoned was sent to Switzerland and Milan). Yet these men continued to carry out important activities on behalf of the insurance company—which did not abandon them—while staying true to their patriotic and then political commitment.

At the height of the Risorgimento, the Veneto management of Generali decided to adopt the Lion of St. Mark as its logo for its business in Italy, instead of the Hapsburg double-headed eagle. The winged lion, emblem of Venice, thus began to be used as a symbol of success also for the company, whose name soon became paired with that of the city.

Before the annexation of Venice to the newborn Kingdom of Italy, however, other events were also witnessed from the windows of the Procuratie Vecchie: one evening in 1858, Richard Wagner—who was sitting as usual at Caffè Lavena, his favourite—was celebrated by the band of the Austrian Navy and that of a Hungarian regiment. That evening the two groups, who were in the square for a concert, in honour of the maestro challenged each other by playing his overtures: to the great surprise and disappointment of the composer, the Venetians did not applaud the performances. Not because they didn't enjoy the music, indeed, Wagner has always been very popular in the city. But because they could not applaud the Austrians, following the dictates of a clandestine proclamation of the Venetian Revolutionary Committee which strictly prohibited "slavish tributes and cowardly insults."

Eventually Venice became Italian and only one year later, in 1867, Giuseppe Garibaldi would look out of a window of the Procuratie Vecchie to greet the crowd which, this time, applauded with no reservations. Today a plaque commemorates the event. After all, five years earlier it had been Leone Pincherle himself, from his Parisian exile, who had requested the famous surgeon Auguste Nélaton to go to the Varignano military complex to treat the general who had been wounded in the Aspromonte region.

Between the end of the nineteenth century and the beginning of the twentieth century, Assicurazioni Generali rolled out an extensive programme of real estate investments, which resulted in the construction of new buildings in various Italian cities, such as Trieste and Rome; in Venice the company made the

Giovanni Battista Dalla Libera, *Venetian Assembly of Rebels against the Austrian Government. Venice will Resist the Austrian at all Costs, 2 April 1849*, late nineteenth century. Museo Correr, Venice.

Marcello Dudovich, *The Venetian Woman*, 1928.

As a woman of vast culture and great spirit, thanks to her high birth and determination, Giustina Renier Michiel became the historical memory of La Serenissima after its fall and was the proudest defender of the Republic and its institutions: "First and foremost, I am venezianissima."

Procuratie building definitively become its "home." During that same period, St. Mark's Square was home to the foundation of the *Bollettino*, the first Italian corporate magazine, still published today.

For the city that period was a season of rebirth and great vitality: with the revival of its history and traditions that had been dormant for decades, the birth of the Lido's seaside époque (which would later become the location of the first and oldest film festival), and the foundation of the Art Biennale. The key players of this season were a number of entrepreneurs and administrators of great vision; some of them sat on the board of directors of Assicurazioni Generali, or chaired it: Nicolò Papadopoli Aldobrandini, entrepreneur and numismatist, member of Parliament and Senator, who implemented modern agrarian reforms in the Polesine area; Pompeo Gherardo Molmenti, author of the timeless *Storia di Venezia nella vita privata* (History of Venice in private life), to whom we owe, among other things, the transfer of Museo Correr to the Procuratie and the location of the Marciana Library in the ancient Libreria del Sansovino; Giuseppe Volpi di Misurata, a highly successful businessman in the fields of international trade, energy and industry, Senator, Minister of Finance, President of Confindustria and of the Venice Biennale; he was the organiser of the first International Exhibition of Cinematographic Art in 1932, which still today awards the Coppa Volpi to the best performers. He was president from 1938 to 1943 until a press campaign broke out describing his company as a "Jewish powerhouse." Volpi resigned after being arrested by the Germans.

The close connection between Generali, Venice and those men who made it great over the last two centuries is also highlighted by some posters made for the company in the 1920s and 1930s by the great master of poster design Marcello Dudovich: his most recurring iconographic themes refer to Venetian settings: a fluttering shawl of a woman looking at the lagoon, the Todaro and winged lion statues in Piazzetta San Marco, a prayer at the *capitello*, and other classic city views.

The twentieth-century "Venetian character" of Assicurazioni Generali is also evident in some specific choices, such as the commissioning from the historic Fortuny fabric company of tapestries to be displayed in the windows of the Procuratie on special occasions; or the continuation of its own nautical club within an ancient squero, with gondolas and other typical boats always present during city events, and in major international events, where they represent the company and Venice; all the way to the most pop among St. Mark's Square symbols: the pigeons, attracted by the food the porters of the Procuratie Vecchie headquarters used to distribute until 1974, forming the AG initials to create an amazing postcard.

The Procuratie Vecchie, the ancient heart of Venice, treasure a small secret: from one of their arches, you can look at the Basilica and the square itself from the proper perspective. St. Mark's Square is known to be a long irregular trapezoid where nothing aligns (even though this certainly does not compromise the overall harmony of the square).

But try positioning yourself at the centre of the fifth arch of the Procuratie Vecchie from the corner of Museo Correr: there you will find a small round bronze seal embedded in the marble flooring. Stand on it and look up again towards St. Mark's Basilica and you'll enjoy a perfectly perpendicular view of the church.

The Procuratie Vecchie are therefore something of an architectural centre of gravity for the square; and Assicurazioni Generali, that today for the first time are making them accessible to the city and to the world, are also turning them into an emotional centre of gravity, rediscovering a new balance.

A NEW START AND AN EXAMPLE

ALDO MAZZOCCO

The restoration project for the monumental complex of the Procuratie Vecchie and Royal Gardens in Venice, promoted and funded by the Generali Group, represents the beginning of a polycentric and carefully planned enhancement of parts of the historic centre of Venice; it will hopefully expand the horizon of urban renovation so as to include new tourist routes, which would complement the conventional and internationally known itineraries (Ponte di Rialto, St. Mark's Basilica, Palazzo Ducale) and, above all, open to a much more local and urban public.

Venice must be experienced with greater awareness of its long and glorious history, and more respect for those who live there. With this in mind, the Generali Group carried out this project, aimed at breathing new life into the functions of the Procuratie Vecchie – Royal Gardens complex.

The new path leading to St. Mark's Square through the renovated Royal Gardens and the open galleries of the Procuratie Nuove, enriched by art exhibitions, provides access to the square from the sea, the latter being the very reason behind the foundation of this amazing and once powerful city.

The restoration and regeneration of the Royal Gardens immediately attracted the attention of the local population, who regained a wonderful piece of their city, which is often hostile to its own inhabitants due to mass tourism. It can be seen as a break in the urban fabric, made of greenery and beautiful architecture, directly in front of the San Marco Basin, from which people can directly access the square without walking around the Marciana Library.

The renovation of the Procuratie Vecchie, an intervention that for over fifteen years all Venetian citizens have longed for, an edifice reflecting the one-thousand-year history of the Serenissima Republic, also represents an important and historically relevant facet of the oldest area of the large square.

The renovation of a medieval structure, which especially on the facade was heavily reconstructed and embellished in the sixteenth century, at the apex of the Republic, culminating with Jacopo Sansovino's final and skilful restoration project, was neither simple nor intuitive. The linear and classically modular facade of the building's body concealed an internal "library-like" structure, with vertical bands that were totally inconsistent with the imposing horizontal arrangement of the facade. Furthermore, many of the internal components had been modified—over the centuries and especially in the early twentieth century—according to a functional logic rather than to a clear architectural design.

The meticulous and philologically accurate reconstruction, combined with fruitful collaboration between David Chipperfield's architecture studio, the Generali Group, and the Superintendence of Architectural Heritage and Landscape of Venice and its Lagoon, led to the inclusion of new vertical paths on the neglected parts of the building; paths which reach the third floor, a large horizontal area where it was possible to accommodate new and elegant spaces, suitable for contemporary use, without sacrificing in any way the spirit of the place or the charm of the medieval and sixteenth-century structure.

Months of painstaking work, also carried out during the agonising period of the pandemic lockdown, made it possible—still under the careful supervision and advice of the Superintendence—to realise a new masterpiece, which now includes the original building, Sansovino's restoration and the work of one of the greatest contemporary architects: the three eras intertwine and are harmoniously integrated.

And last but not least, thanks to the expertise of the Generali Real Estate team, the Procuratie Vecchie are nowadays a hallmark for ensuring that buildings, even those conceived centuries ago, meet the proper levels of sustainability.

The new structure includes, among other areas, one of the most stunning and modern spaces for conferences and concerts in the city; it will ensure the future participation of the Procuratie Vecchie in Venice's urban life.

It will now be the task of the Generali Group and The Human Safety Net Foundation, that physically inhabits the building, to instil the vital spirit that will make the Procuratie Vecchie a new source of energy in St. Mark's Square, bringing another piece of Venice back to the centre of a network of "people who help people," in line with The Human Safety Net's mission.

MEDIATING BETWEEN PAST, PRESENT AND FUTURE

DAVID CHIPPERFIELD

in conversation with

LUCA MOLINARI

Luca M. I would like to start by asking you what is your relationship with Venice. You have had such an intense relationship with Venice over the last fifteen years or more, whether curating the Biennale, working on the San Michele cemetery which you partly redesigned, and now with the Procuratie Vecchie on St. Mark's Square. You have worked on some key parts of the city.

David C. I suspect I have a similarly romantic relationship to Venice as many others. Like other architects or lovers of architecture, this relationship is rooted in the feeling that Venice is a mysterious triumph of architecture both over nature and with nature. It's a very unusual situation where nature and architecture are both winners, both improved by the presence of the other. Venice is the most natural of places as well as the most artificial, having been founded where there is no land. Venice is a demonstration of architecture performing at a very high level, not only on an individual basis, building by building, but also as a collective achievement. The particular context of St. Mark's Square is all the more interesting for being nearly the only moment where formality is imposed into the informality of the organic form of the city which is mostly designed in negotiation with nature.

Venice is the most natural of places as well as the most artificial, having been founded where there is no land.

It is true that I have had a fairly long-standing relationship with Venice through various projects. My relationship with the city is one of fondness, as well as of deep concern about its future. Tourism in the city, like its beauty, is demonstrated in the extreme. Venice is at risk of becoming entirely dominated by tourism and shopping, leading towards the sanitisation of the centre and a loss of dynamism, diversity, vitality and activity—the qualities for which we love cities. This problem can certainly be found elsewhere too, but perhaps nowhere more explicitly than in Venice. .

Luca M. This is very interesting because while listening to your reflections on Venice, I was thinking that when a city loses its dynamism it becomes less organic, and its capability of being a living body deteriorates. By this I mean a city's capacity to react and to change, to be very flexible in response to different kinds of communities and needs and desires which emerge over time. If you work and stress the city in only one predominant direction, which in this case is leisure and tourism, you end up crystalising it. As a result, the city risks losing its wholeness, because the city is a living body that must change, die and be born again every day, in a completely non-strategic way, let's say.

David C. The problem is that there is also a more hidden danger that impacts on our wider activities as citizens. Often we find that if you have a tourism-focused economy, everything else tends to become neglected by the administration and commerce. There is an assumption that you do not need to think about careers for young people in the city because it is simply assumed that they are going to work in hospitality. But this is not a truly sustainable model and it does not support long-term quality of life for inhabitants. This is something we are taking into consideration in Galicia where our non-profit, Fundación RIA is working on pilot projects with the support of the regional government. As a city, Santiago has some similar issues to Venice. Luckily, Galicia is not dominated by tourism yet and it is mostly related to religious pilgrimage, but these aspects are a concern. What we sense is that the big danger is not tourism in itself, it's that other activities and industries that keep an area self-sufficient and facilitate daily life are suppressed or receive less investment in favour of the tourist industry.

13th International Architecture Exhibition at the Venice Biennale titled *Common Ground*, directed by David Chipperfield, 2012.

Luca M. I totally agree. There is need for a better vision for our cities. Returning to St. Mark's Square and the relationship between architecture and nature, this place strikes me as a perfect merging of those two visions because, as you know, St. Mark's Square was designed to be seen from the sea by those arriving by boat, therefore its primary side was along the waterfront. When there was *acqua alta*, the sea and the square merged together creating a unique landscape, somewhat dangerous and magical.

> When there was *acqua alta*, the sea and the square merged together creating a unique landscape, somewhat dangerous and magical.

The square is a perfect relationship between formal and informal, between a theatrical representation of power and the communities floating around it and shaping it. Sometimes people forget that, behind the static facade you have an architecture that is a living everchanging body, as the Procuratie Vecchie demonstrate. What are your thoughts on being the first architect in one hundred and fifty years to be working on a large portion of this square? Because, on the one hand, you're working on a typical symbol, an archetype, a postcard, let's say, which is a kind of fixed image, but on the other, this project is also meant as a rebirth, to help the square step away from stereotype and generate another kind of vision and activities.

David C. Yes, you are absolutely right. St. Mark's Square is very theatrical, an aspect that does not diminish its architectural robustness but that confirms it draws on theatrical qualities to create an extraordinary setting. It is very interesting, as you said, if you leave the square and look at the back facade of the Procuratie Vecchie, which is much more expressive. While the frontages on the square are uncompromising and rigid, the back is totally flexible and highly varied. It's all sorts of things—perhaps some might even call it a mess—but I see it as a mediation between the two conditions of the whole city: the formal and the organic. When you say that we are working on St. Mark's Square, I'm tempted to say it's not strictly true because we did not touch St. Mark's Square, we hardly even affected the facades that enclose it. On the other hand, I think you can say that we are indirectly working on the square in a softer sense. What is so positive about the reoccupation of the Procuratie Vecchie building is that it encompasses the recuperation of activity. It's great that we can support Generali in this endeavour to re-energise the city centre. As architects, we do this through a response to the physical substance. Our work begins behind the facade, on the organisation of space behind it.

> These interventions on the original building now form part of its history, so what we are trying to do is to resolve the more incongruous modifications, treat the neglected fabric and give back some stability and logic to the complex as a whole, while also being respectful of its long history.

The internal hardware of the Procuratie Vecchie has, as you say, been modified and changed over time into a beehive of structures. While there is a strong horizontality to the Procuratie Vecchie from the outside, internally it was originally structured vertically into several "slices," each one a unit for a Procurator. This then became a problem in more recent centuries when the building housed other administrative functions that required more horizontal internal connections and led to the disintegration of the verticality in parts. The morphology of the building has been in a crisis several times throughout its history, each change of use leaving its trace in the internal arrangement and fabric of the building. These interventions on the original building now are part of its history, so what we are trying to do is to resolve the more incongruous modifications, treat the neglected fabric and give back some stability and logic to the complex as a whole, while also being respectful of its long history. We have to maintain a level of intellectual and professional independence to navigate this process effectively, mediating between the client, the city and its history.

Luca M. Yes, it's a very delicate balance, I agree with you. And the approach you chose was very clear from the beginning of the competition. Could you go into detail about your project? I find your reflection on the horizontal versus vertical quality very interesting, as well as the fact that you had to harmonise those unsolved layers. There are now two new staircases and the top floor has become part of the new project. There's a new conference space, a new exhibition space, and a relation has been established with the roof. This part of the building has probably become the key element in the definition of the contemporary intervention. Could you tell us more about these aspects?

David C. We enjoy working on restoration projects not as restoration experts but as modern architects. I realise this is quite unusual but we are fascinated by working with existing and historic buildings. When you design a new building you strive to find meaning and a relationship with the surrounding community and its context from within the confines of your client's interests and brief. What is interesting with cultural institutions and historic buildings, even if they are only a few decades old, is that these buildings already have a sense of common ownership. We feel that such buildings belong to all of us, we have affection for them and they carry meaning, which means that the dialogue around them is heightened, often in a positive way.

Form should not follow function—function is subjective, it is not a scientific certainty and must adjust to the limitations and opportunities of the building.

The Procuratie Vecchie building is deeply embedded in its Venetian context, almost becoming a part of its nature, and that's why people have affection for it. The dialogue when you are working on such a building is fascinating and requires you to find a relationship between the programme and the fabric. There must always be flexibility when discussing the programme. Form should not follow function—function is subjective, it is not a scientific certainty and must adjust to the limitations and opportunities of the building. Identifying those hard boundaries, the irremovable character, the singular nature, as well as the softer spaces that are more malleable is our responsibility as architects. Given the public dimension of Generali's mission for the site, we were looking to find the softer areas to accommodate some larger spaces, which led us to the top of the building.

To demolish walls on the lower levels would be against the building's morphology so it was natural for us to work with the less defined character of the top of the building and create a conference space there. Our process allowed us the flexibility to respond to the fabric, to clarify, solidify, confirm and protect what needs to be treasured, and to enjoy those places where you might be able to find more space for programmatic and architectural opportunities.

Luca M. I totally agree with what you say about the word "function." It was a keyword, almost adogma, for early avant-gardists, but nowadays it no longer has much meaning. I think "purpose" is more useful as it brings us to a deeper level and to a vision for the building, which after all can outlive its original functions. When I was a student, one of my university professors once said: "good architecture survives function." This is evident everywhere. So many churches have become museums, for example. And I think that this is very clear in the work you have done on this building, and in the projects you have carried out over the last thirty years, whether in Berlin or London: projects where you have really dealt with the existing conditions, yet thinking as a contemporary architect, a lucid modern architect. And I can see clearly the approach, the methodology you applied, which is very strong. Earlier you talked about Venice and the quality of the city. But what about its future, its destiny? As Director of M9 Museum of the Twentieth Century I spend plenty of time in Venice and there's much discussion about its future. There are interesting occasions involving several institutions, foundations, artists and opening spaces, and there's an ongoing lively debate about the relations between tech, art and science. Venice is experiencing a very interesting season, no longer being just a stage for exhibitions or events but rather opening discussions about the next phase of the city without being too futuristic. What do think would be interesting for a city like Venice at this moment?

Extension of the San Michele in Isola Cemetery, Venice – David Chipperfield Architects Milan.

David C. It's really easy: young people. In the past cities always felt that the solution to their revival would be to focus on attracting large-scale investments and big companies, showing a tendency to neglect the importance of daily quality of life of young people and the energy they bring. For cities like Venice you have to think about how to keep, or lure back, young people to live and work there. What is clear is that it cannot rely on tourism alone.
Berlin is a good example; it has become such an interesting place to be because of its capacity to support and inspire a sustainable quality of life for young people.
How can Venice learn from this? The city must support industries that provide meaningful work beyond tourism, it must create affordable working and living spaces, and ensure the provision of key services and facilities. The future is to go back to those basics, to make sure that these are places that function for daily life first and foremost. The rest follows.

Luca M. I totally agree. And my last question is about your foundation in Galicia, one of the most beautiful places in Spain. I was reading about the work Fundación RIA is doing on territories and communities. I would like to know more about the foundation, because that seems to be another way to use your architectural skills and to give something back.

David C. In some ways it has been an accidental process. My family and I have been spending time in Galicia over the last thirty years and I have always wanted to give something back to the place. I was fortunate to be approached by the President of the Region some years ago and asked for advice on how to consider issues of ugly development and on the condition of the towns and villages throughout the region. It soon became clear to me that we needed to look at the underlying issues, that it was of no use to look at the built environment in isolation, and that we were to consider the matter within the context of wider urban planning, and social and environmental issues. To address the issue of empty buildings you must address the lack of opportunities, which is the reason why people left in the first place. So five years ago we initiated a study which has now become a non-profit foundation, using our architectural skills to mediate issues between stakeholders and governance bodies, managing pilot projects and supporting sustainable industries.

> To address the issue of empty buildings you must address the lack of opportunities, which is the reason why people left in the first place.

One of the key areas we are looking at is traffic—how it affects the quality of life in towns and villages, the mobility between places, the impact on local ecosystems and social support networks. Like in many places, the role of coherent planning is underestimated or under resourced.
We also work with the local communities and enterprises, the commercial sector, fishing sector and forestry sector, and with the three universities, in Vigo, A Coruña and Santiago. The foundation is made up of a team of architects: we have not built a single piece of architecture but we feel passionately about these issues and the role that we can play as an independent agency in improving the environment of the region. I think the architectural profession is really struggling to define its social role within the confines of conventional practice but it is clear that we must become more and more dynamic in the way we work.

Luca M. It's an amazing challenge. It seems that the context was ready for this to happen, open to the idea of working with an agency, manifesting a growing desire among the communities and an economic need for change. Young people need hope in the future in order to carry out their projects, otherwise they leave. They won't wait. So I agree with you, we must build opportunities, not just empty buildings.

David C. I think we can see in Generali's ambitions with the Procuratie Vecchie project an important shift taking place, promoting the centre of Venice as a place of work, with its co-working spaces and residency programme.
The ambition to fill St. Mark's Square with more daily life and more diverse activities gives me hope for the future, and I hope it will for young people of Venice too.

FABRIC OF HISTORY

GIUSEPPE ZAMPIERI

CRISTIANO BILLIA

The Uniqueness of the Whole Every worksite represents the implementation of an idea that may involve operations for the realisation of a new edifice or operations for the recovery of an existing one, or indeed a combination of both.
A worksite like that of the *fabric* of the Procuratie Vecchie, for the most part owned by Generali, where the historic Venetian edifice is composed of parts which in turn are composed of spaces of varying typologies and degrees of conservation, all concealed behind one single continuous façade is complicated and presents an intricate history. This worksite required not only a particular set up and a range of equipment in order to carry out a variety of operations, but also needed a method of strategies and approaches to determine different types and levels of operations aimed at carrying out acts of maintenance, restoration, refurb and construction.

All operations on a delicate historic edifice such as the Procuratie Vecchie were carried out almost like a surgical operation, performed with the aim of rehabilitating the body of the *fabric* as a true architectural organism.

The Greek etymology of the word *surgery* [*chirurgia* in Italian] indicates operating by hand and so, just as in an operating theatre one intervenes on a body and its organs to preserve the entire organism, so on the worksite we work on the body of the *fabric* and its parts, both manually and with instruments, in order to recuperate the entire architectural system while respecting its constitution and conformation, its development and evolution.

The various parts of the body of the *fabric* were treated almost as organs and the operations were carried out using various surgical techniques, whilst never losing sight of the architectural organism as a whole.

The operations adopted for the internal circulatory organs such as the stairs between the courtyards—Corte Ca' Bardellini, Corte dell'Arco Celeste, Corte del Cavalletto, Corte Ca' Maruzzi and Corte Ca' da Riva—are reminiscent of general surgery, through operations of reconstruction on all levels. The operations for the extended organs such as the walls bring to mind plastic surgery, through interventions of reconstruction for both aesthetic and functional purposes, mainly in the attic space on the third level.

The operations on the other complex organs with more stratifications required the highest level of care and perfection, and recall highly-specialised surgery because they are more delicate and complex, carried out through the reconstruction of the supporting elements of the internal cavities, mainly on the first and second level of the architectural organism.

Right from the start, this project identified different degrees and typologies of methods and systems for the surgical operations on the different parts of the body of the *fabric*, according to different needs and purposes, and the worksite progressed from one area to another until the whole body of the Procuratie Vecchie *fabric* was involved.

The project and the worksite evolved continuously, as a result of the fusion of the various constituent parts of the historic edifice in the context of a unified architectural organism, seeking the implementation of an idea of the uniqueness of the whole.

A Meeting of Directions

The worksite for the renovation of the *fabric* of the Procuratie Vecchie—a composite and heterogeneous architectural organism—challenged the project's capacity for resilience in accommodating the evolution and transformation of the worksite, withstanding the pressures and tensions and responding to the unexpected and the unpredictable.

These challenges were evident from the beginning of the works that Generali Real Estate assigned to the Tonon firm from Vittorio Veneto in November 2016; during the interventions, from March 2017, with the Rizzani De Eccher company from Pozzuolo del Friuli; through the suspension of the works from March to May 2020 due to Covid-19; ending in March 2022 when they were completed.

The fact that the architectural, structural and plant engineering interventions aimed at safeguarding the historic edifice were successful can be attributed to all the players involved, from the development of the project and the organisation of the worksite to the combined action in response to expected conditions and to unexpected situations.

Although works management and artistic direction have different functions, maintaining a continuous dialogue was essential for the outcome of the delicate interventions on the historic edifice, as was the constant dialogue with the Superintendency of Archaeology, Fine Arts and Landscape for Venice and Laguna (DGABAP) and the Ministry of Culture (MIC) in Rome.

On the one hand the works management, with the integrated engineering specialised group, Artelia Italia in Milan—from November 2016 to April 2020—and with the integrated design group TA Architettura in Mestre—from April 2020 to April 2022—was tasked with closely following the interventions on the worksite, certifying their correct execution and realisation, and issuing the appropriate instructions and indications.

On the previous page
Enfilade of arches at level three.

Facing page
View from oculus at level three.

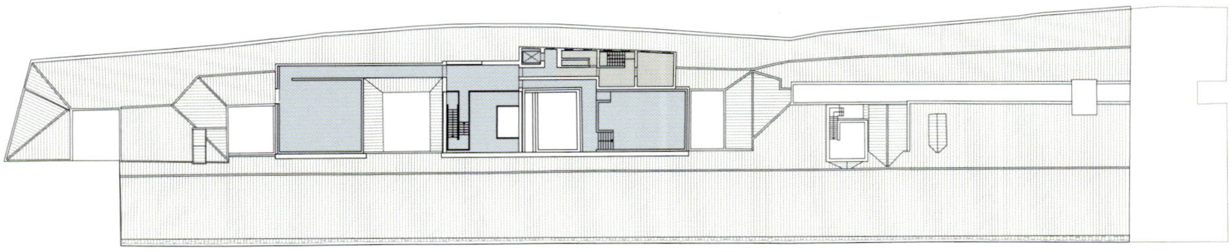

Fourth floor plan

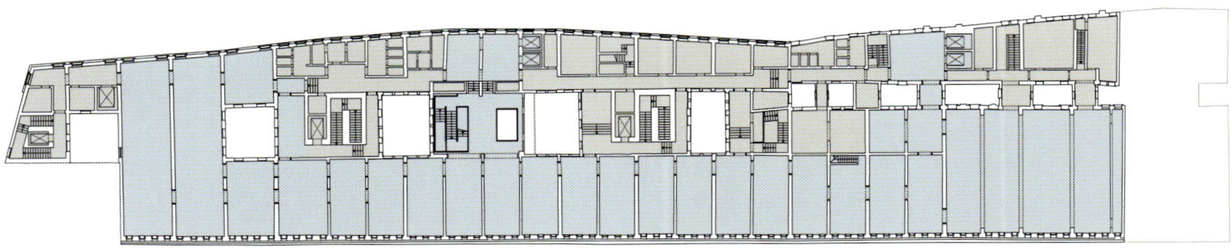

Third floor plan

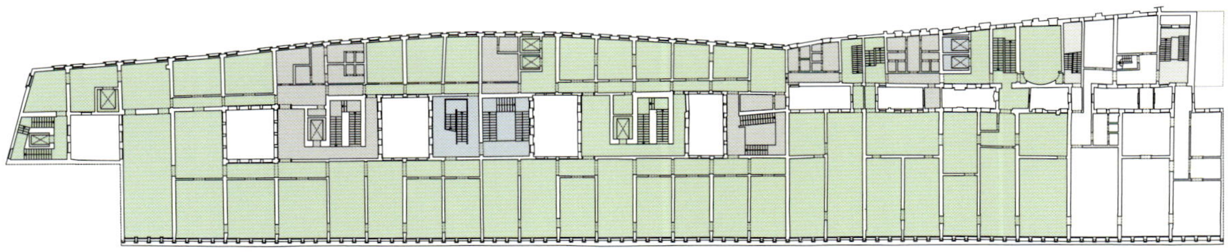

Second floor plan

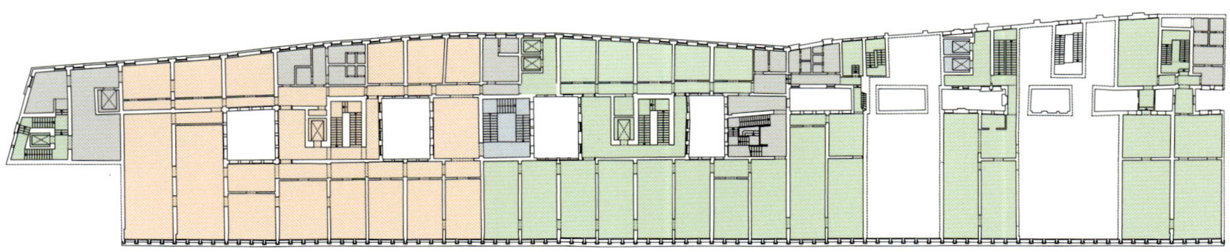

First floor plan

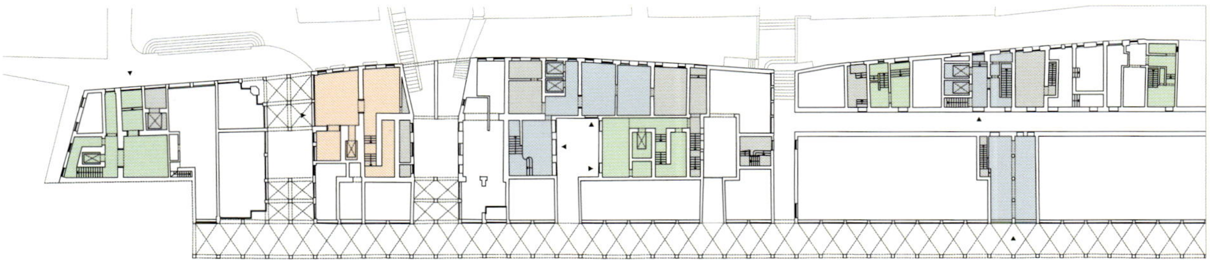

Ground floor plan

The Human Safety Net

Assicurazioni Generali Offices

Offices

Services

Facing page
Section model of all levels.

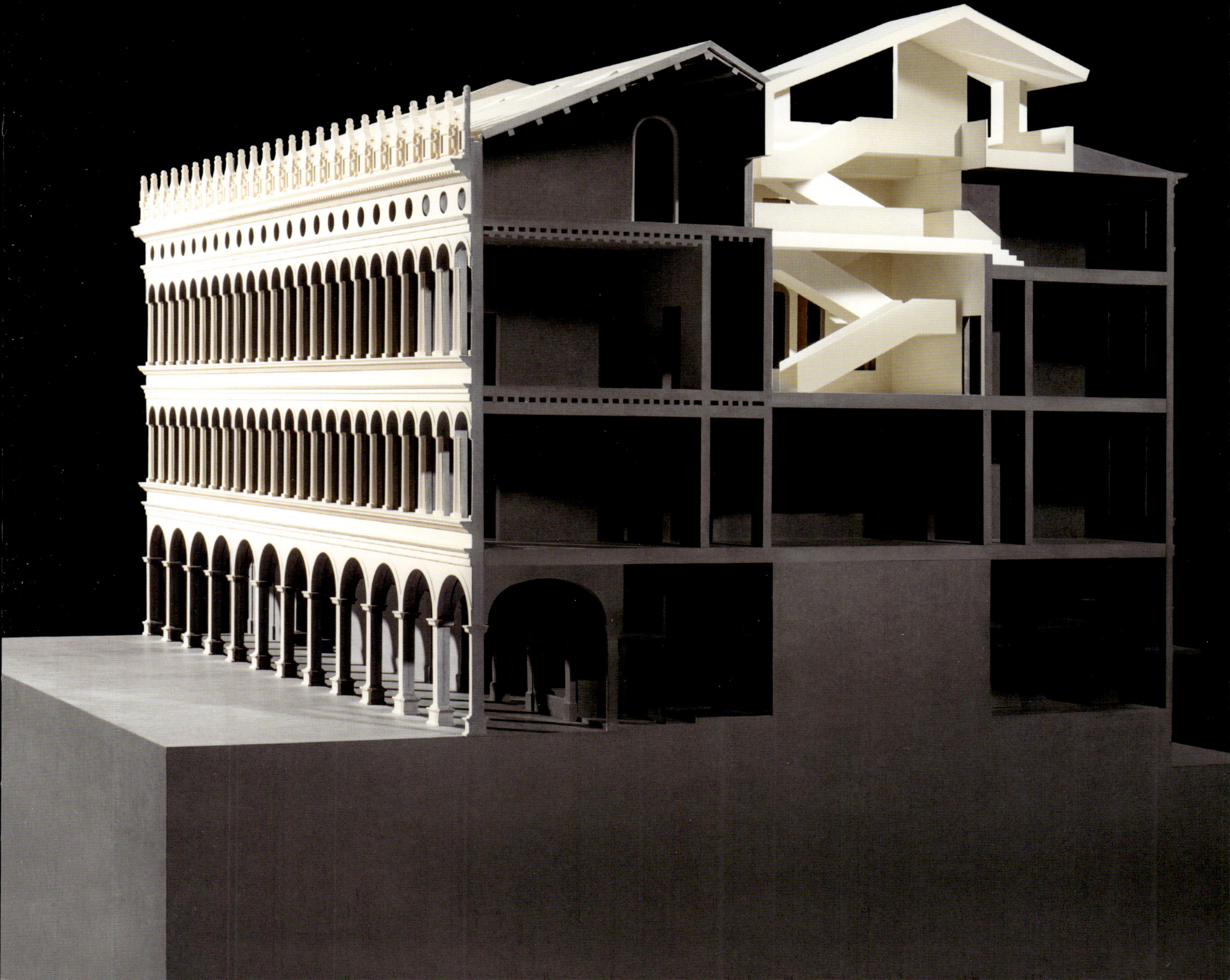

On the other hand, the artistic direction—David Chipperfield Architects in Milan—from January 2019 to March 2022—was tasked with guaranteeing and ensuring compliance with the project's aims and advising and suggesting in close collaboration with the works management. Both the works management and the artistic direction benefited from a process of mutual exchange in a virtuous circle, each time supplementing what was lacking and/or insufficient and adding what was useful and/or necessary.

On the worksite, all the players involved understood the necessity to consider the project not as inherited or innate, but as mutable and dynamic, and that the complex of tasks and responsabilities of supervision, direction and management in the context of project and worksite planning required a highly integrated approach for the maintenance, restoration and refurb of the Procuratie Vecchie building.

The managerial and supervisory role, by the Generali RE group—from the beginning of the project to its completion—as well as the administrative, organisational, operational and implementational functions, enabled a course of action to be developed that was able to connect the ideal and the theoretical with the real and the concrete, a direction along which the execution of the project and its realisation on the worksite could progress, sensitively and efficiently, through a ceaseless juxtaposition of orientations, always aimed at a continual meeting of directions.

Between Worksite and Project

The project for the execution and realisation of the works envisaged in the *fabric* of the Procuratie Vecchie building consisted essentially of a set of recommendations and suggestions about how to intervene and operate on the worksite, expressed through ideas and proposals defined abstractly, accompanied by specific studies and research, and concretely, to determine all the possibilities of implementing and realising interventions and operations.

The guidelines that sprang from the project—developed to establish suitable processes and systems rather than standard norms and solutions—became of fundamental importance for the implementation of the interventions, a set of principles and actions that was continually updated on the basis of the knowledge acquired as the worksite progressed.

Just as the Latin etymology of the locution *modus operandi* refers to the set of actions aimed at planning and carrying out a series of interventions, so the project defined a way of working with the worksite that could be easily and conveniently adapted to the needs that arose as the worksite progressed, determining the most appropriate actions—reconstructive measures were requested or, in other places, appropriate therapeutic measures—all intended to restore efficiency and improve functionality in relation to the need for partial or total recovery of the parts of the *fabric* that had suffered trauma or neglect.

The set of actions defined and employed for the interventions involved revealing parts that were previously hidden or inaccessible, repairing deteriorated or weakened parts that compromised the integrity or functionality, and reworking parts using techniques and themes that drew on the essence of the old to give meaning to the new. This method was applied especially in relation to the restoration of the *fabric* on the decorative elements of the walls on levels one and two, from March 2019 to March 2020, to the renovation of the flooring of levels one and two, from September 2019 to January 2021; to the reinforcement of the structures on levels one and two from, November 2019 to December 2020; to the installation of the ceilings, from November 2020 to July 2021.

The meaning of the Italian word for worksite, *cantiere*, refers to the support structures used for shipbuilding and, in many ways, the *cantiere* of the Procuratie Vecchie in turn supported the consolidation of the project through a retroactive process of fine-tuning, guiding the approach and action as the conditions and circumstances were revealed.

This process occurred especially in relation to the interventions of construction and fabrication of the secondary stairs, from September 2019 to October 2021; to the extension and continuation of the main staircases, from July 2021 to February 2022; to the construction of the central volume, from October 2020 to December 2021; to the placement and adaption of the roofs and terraces, from August 2020 to March 2022; to the demolition and construction of the multipurpose space, from September 2020 to October 2021; and to the insertion and integration of the stone portals, from January to April 2021.

The *fabric* of the Procuratie Vecchie had the opportunity to be modified and adapted, while in the process reconfirming and validating its own substantive authority, finding suitable solutions in a continuous back and forth of action and reaction, between worksite and project.

Certainty in Uncertainty

The need to understand the viability of the project directly on the *fabric* of the Procuratie Vecchie on the one hand, and the need to assess the reality of the worksite indirectly from the perspective of the architectural organism on the other, enabled the project to be continuously and conversely evaluated through the worksite.

Even if the architectural organism sometimes led to unexpected solutions, changes of direction and sudden twists, the established goal was however maintained, following a clear pathway traced by the project. Partial modifications to the project, considered as a complementary guide and a conceptual constraint, were a constant of the worksite, considered the architectural organism as a fundamental guide and a physical constraint, suggesting modifications to what had previously been established in relation to both specific and general aspects. These modifications—realised in constant collaboration with Generali Real Estate Group—occurred above all in relation to revisions of the detailed design, from August to October 2018; to the integrations of the detailed design, from October 2018 to May 2019; to the variations on the auditorium and entrances, from September 2020 to January 2021; and also as a consequence of the extraordinarily high tides experienced in 2019 when on twenty-eight occasions the sea level exceeded the limit of 110 cm (flooding 12% of Venice) leading to further changes to the project.

Despite the initial uncertainties when the project was first drafted, trust in the ideas was maintained for the duration of the worksite, even if there was a continuous fluctuation between the resolution of ambiguities and the emergence of problems, and thanks to the mixture of actions suggested by the project and reactions required by the worksite, it was possible in the end to find solutions that were more solid and certain.

The actions of completion and replacement, as well as the those of addition and subtraction envisaged by the project, merged together on the worksite with actions of innovation and conservation.

The worksite and the project were reciprocally inspired and enriched by a continuous dialogue, with the ultimate objective of achieving an optimal renovation of the architectural organism.

During each phase, area and part of the body of the architectural organism, the worksite selected and evaluated the operations of the project that needed to be implemented, leading to choices and decisions to be made along the way in a dynamic process that offered the chance to combine the hypothesised initiatives to obtain a wider range of solutions.

The ultimate ambition in this process was to integrate the history of the edifice in a discerning project, instead of fossilising it in a celebratory project, and avoiding reproduction on the one hand and anything formulaic on the other. At the same time, the project was integrated into the worksite through the renewal of a complex architectural organism with its own logic, ensuring that the *fabric* of the Procuratie Vecchie itself became the subject of its own story and determination.

The worksite and the project did not work for mutual exclusion, moving in opposite directions, but rather worked to overlap each other as complementary phenomena: two forces tempered by the challenges that appeared with the certainty of the result in the midst of uncertainty.

Following pages
Restorated rooms at level one.

Pages 62-63
Restorated rooms at level two.

INTONATURA

A CONSTRUCTION SITE

GUIDO GUIDI

There is a small difference between working for oneself and working for clients; when it comes to clients, you have to deliver a job, so you are encouraged "to do," while if you work for yourself, you tend to waste time, never completing what you're doing... So, all clients are welcome, but provided that they are smart enough to allow you—within the framework of a project—to do what you are interested in.

Venice is not photogenic; or... it's too photogenic.
Venice has already been photographed by many tourists. During this photoshoot, I don't have to take pictures of Venice or St. Mark's Square... but even if I were to photograph St. Mark's Square, I could also find some moments there, corners that have never been captured.
You either take pictures... the same ones everyone takes *ad nauseam*, or go... and find somewhat invisible things, that others have overlooked.
It is impossible to have seen everything. It is not true that photographers have shot everything, that there is nothing left to capture any more, because the world shifts and we also change, as men and as photographers; reality is always new, even if it refers to past forms.

I don't photograph the things that will be. Now there is this phase, this moment; in a year, this place perhaps will be different and later will change again... Will there be someone who modifies it, who wants to change it again? Will there still be someone who takes care of it, or will it be neglected? We don't know how the story ends.
I photograph what can be seen, not in a global sense... there is no global vision, because then it would be a complete, definitive vision, rather than a vision in transit.
The detail symbolises the whole; the whole can be boring because you no longer know which way to look, but a detail is always mysterious and intriguing.*

* Excerpts from *Visions in Transit* by Marlon Sartore, a video-interview made during a photoshoot by Guido Guidi of the construction sites of the Procuratie Vecchie and the Royal Gardens of Venice.

GIORGIO

F 10

LEGNO
CER 17.02.01

Promatect-H,ETA 06/0206-fact 02.22-11-17

NO
NT.

GRANIGLIATO
Grigolin MIXCEM PRONTO
Grigolin MIXCEM PRONTO

RESTORING HARMONY. THE VENICE GARDENS FOUNDATION AND THE ROYAL GARDENS OF VENICE

ADELE RE REBAUDENGO

The Venice Gardens Foundation, that I am honored to chair, was founded in Venice in 2014, with the objective of preserving and enhancing parks, gardens, as well as historical and cultural assets. The Foundation promotes, develops, and implements projects aimed at safeguarding the botanical and artistic heritage, while recognising the fundamental role that these spaces play in the social and community context, fostering a harmonious accord between the human spirit and nature.

> The core value and goal of these projects is to promote harmony between all living beings, using the right words, that is, precise, symbolic, and evocative terms, in order to reach a more natural form of understanding.

All the sites restored by the Foundation are directly managed and preserved by their own gardeners, through specific programmes that combine ancient knowledge and new techniques. Included in the Association of the International Private Committees for the Safeguarding of Venice and in the National Research Registry of the Ministry of Education, University, and Research, the Venice Gardens Foundation is thus engaged in developing and implementing studies aimed at innovation as well as the sustainable and responsible management of environmental assets, while offering relevant training courses.

The core value and goal of these projects is to promote harmony between all living beings, using the right words, that is, precise, symbolic, and evocative terms, in order to reach a more natural form of understanding. In line with the fundamental principles of patronage, there is also room for works of art closely related to the essence and life of the gardens.

In view of these values, the Venice Gardens Foundation supervised and implemented, from 2014 to 2019, the renovation of the Royal Gardens of Venice. On the one hand, the work influenced the urban and architectural principles and themes that gave life to the nineteenth-century project, and on the other, it restored the balance between those parts and areas that shape the face of the city. Today the Gardens—which are vital, prosperous, exuberant, but also sober, with plants from various parts of the world—represent an important botanical dimension of hospitality, congenial to the spirit of Venice.

The Napoleonic Gardens, now reconnected to St. Mark's Square, extend over an area of about five thousand square metres, overlooking the San Marco Basin, and are surrounded by canals which also look out on the Museo Correr, the Imperial Chambers of the Royal Palace, the National Archaeological Museum, and the Marciana National Library.

Since the 1950s, the Royal Gardens, of great value and a source of pride for the city throughout the nineteenth century, had progressively lost their balanced relationship with the adjacent buildings, and for some decades had been in such a state of neglect to make their original geometry and architecture almost unrecognisable. The neoclassical Pavilion, built by architect Lorenzo Santi between 1816 and 1817, showed evident structural defects, while the nineteenth-century cast-iron pergola, the gate, and the historic drawbridge fell into disrepair, as well as the incongruous structures built over time inside the garden.

To halt the progressive deterioration of a site of such noteworthy historical and environmental interest, in December 2014, the Venice Gardens Foundation was commissioned by the State Property Office and the City of Venice to renovate and subsequently safeguard the Monumental Royal Gardens Complex.

Reopened to the public in December 2019, the Royal Gardens—luxuriant and with a wealth of unexpected perspectives—have regained, thanks to the visionary project carried out by landscape architect Paolo Pejrone, their formal value and botanical complexity, again taking centre stage in the city. This was a conservative project, in terms of the design and architecture of the garden, intentionally respectful of the historical evolution of the site (whit an in-depth analysis of the nineteenth-century "Italian garden" flowerbeds), but also innovative and experimental from a botanical and gardening viewpoint, as it strove to achieve the greatest possible freedom and exuberance.

The architectural refurbishment, assigned by the Foundation to architect Alberto Torsello (who partly reused projects by architects Carlo Aymonino and Gabriella Barbini), respected the historical stratification, paying attention to the original design of the garden and the nearby *Cafehaus*. This complex refurbishment also required, as a preliminary work, the demolition of the above-mentioned incongruous buildings, including the reinforced concrete bunker dating back to World War II.

SCOMENZERA
SACAIM
SACAIM

This was a conservative project, in terms of the design and architecture of the garden, intentionally respectful of the historical evolution of the site (whit an in-depth analysis of the nineteenth-century "Italian garden" flowerbeds).

In terms of project implementation, the Venice Gardens Foundation signed a partnership agreement with Assicurazioni Generali, with the common aim of restoring an important historical and artistic site of the Marciana Area.

Botanical Renovation

The Gardens have been redesigned to become a symbol of abundance and luxuriance, a rich and lavish venue, full of flowers, but above all composed of leaves, shade, and shimmering transparent views; the select species include evergreen plants along the foundations, as well as compact bushes of laurels, pittosporums, euonymuses, and silverberries almost creating a sort of vegetable dune, a frontline bulwark against the winds and sea spray; here and there are Mastic trees (*Pistacia lentiscus*) and Japanese Clerodendrums (*Clerodendrum trichotomum*) to enliven and lighten the vegetation, Plumbago (*Plumbago capensis*) climbing freely among the evergreens, and small groups of Osmanthus (*Osmanthus fragrans*) that provide fragrance during autumn.

On the eastern side of the garden, the existing holm oaks have been increased to form a large, dense, compact, and evergreen hedge, with a cluster of plants in the middle, closing the pergola in perspective, whereas at the opposite end, to the west, a bamboo forest hosts plants of different varieties and sizes (including *Phyllostachys viridiglaucescens* and *Phyllosta-chys metake*): the latter is a "new" feature in line with the curiosity and botanical hospitality that have always characterised Venice and this garden in particular.

Along the balcony overlooking the Rio dei Giardini, in order to accentuate the idea of a green border surrounding the garden, which protects it and gives it unity, there are large terracotta pots containing pomegranates, figs, jujubes, shiny *viburnums*, Feijoas (*Acca sellowiana*), and bitter oranges, a symbol of the ancient potted citruses that were once cultivated in the town of Stra (near Venice) and carried away every year by water, in the summer, to the Royal Gardens. The large pergola, which represents the central element of the composition and is a typical Hapsburg feature, included in all gardens of Bohemia and Moravia from which the gardeners of the Empire originated, is now covered with numerous varieties of *Wisteria sinensis* and *Wisteria floribunda* and, at the intersection with the orthogonal avenue leading to the drawbridge and its extremities, with dense bushes of *Bignonia ricasoliana* or "Contessa Sara," which blooms in late summer and fall.

In the four central parterres, large scrubs of *Agapanthus umbellatus* and imposing "Queen Mum" *Agapanthus*, as well as *Farfugium japonicum* and iris from Dalmatia (*Iris dalmatica*) and Florence (*Iris florentina*), all with evergreen leaves, surround a small grove of *Tetrapanax papyrifer*, with its large grey-green velvety leaves, and some "Général Schablikine" roses. All around them, the remaining eight flowerbeds carry on with the theme of bordering *agapanthus* and *farfugium*, which gives way, as the first shadows of the sophores fall, to groups of myrtles (*Myrtus communis*) and *Hydrangea paniculata*; at the edges of the long pergola are "Annabelle" *Hydrangea arborescens*, which gently filter light along the shaded path, separating it from the rest of the garden and making this space more intimate and evocative.

At its foot, to fill the borders of the walkway, *Liriope muscari* and *Ruscus racemosus* create a soft and fresh evergreen carpet. The whole composition is completed by a widespread and light carpet of bulbous plants (in particular, varieties of *Narcissus* and *Tulipa*). Alongside the long-standing tall trees, numerous specimens of *Sophora japonica*, two large camphor trees (*Cinnamomum camphora*), and two *Pterocarya fraxinifolia* were planted.

The Royal Gardens of Venice originate within the framework of Napoleon's reform project of the Marciana Area, with the decision, made official on 11 January 1807, by decree of Napoleon Bonaparte, to turn the Procuratie Nuove into the new headquarters of the Royal Palace.

History of the Royal Gardens: Origins and Transformations[1]

The Royal Gardens of Venice originate within the framework of Napoleon's reform project of the Marciana Area, with the decision, made official on 11 January 1807, by decree of Napoleon Bonaparte, to turn the Procuratie Nuove into the new headquarters of the Royal Palace.

Architect Giovanni Antonio Antolini, who was summoned to Venice in 1806, presented the first projects for the residence: it consisted of a new building overlooking the San Marco Basin, which was not completed, and a garden in the space between the Procuratie and the lagoon, in place of the Terranova storehouses, dating back to the fourteenth century.

Viceroy Eugène de Beauharnais modified Antolini's project and opted for the construction of a monumental new building, the so-called Napoleonic Wing, which would have occupied, in the square, the area of the church of San Geminiano. He instead accepted the project of a garden, which would have allowed for a visual and direct connection with the San Marco Basin. Having demolished the storehouses and shops on site, in 1810, architect Giuseppe Maria Soli started the preliminary works in the garden, e.g. the construction of a stone balustrade and a wooden bridge to provide access from the palace.

After the Austrians returned to the city in 1814, architect Lorenzo Santi (1783–1839) became the new director of the works for the Royal Palace. Born in Siena, he had studied in Rome, where he met Canova, who in 1809 recommended him to oversee the work of the Venetian residence as a draftsman.

In 1815, with the demolition of the bridges over the Rio della Luna, which interrupted the connection with Calle Vallaresso, the garden was isolated from the city, but a drawbridge built over a small internal river provided direct access from the palace, also allowing gondolas to navigate the canals. The entire area was enclosed by a stone balustrade, and in 1816, between the garden and the Riva leading to the Piazzetta di San Marco, a majestic iron gate was placed by the blacksmiths Pietro Acerboni and Daniele Pellanda. Santi gave the garden its final form, creating a tree-lined avenue overlooking the San Marco Basin, "Italian-style" geometric parterres, and two "English-style" groves at each end, whose trees, flowering plants, and potted citruses came from the Royal Park in Stra.

Between 1815 and 1817 the architect finally built a greenhouse on the Ponte della Zecca and, at the end of the new avenue, a new neoclassical pavilion, the *Cafehaus*, whose elaborate sculptural decorations were completed in 1819. In the mid-nineteenth century, the geometric layout of the flowerbeds was replaced by a design with smoother lines, according to "English" taste, very popular in Europe at that time, which essentially remained unchanged up until World War II. In 1857, Emperor Franz Joseph, in an attempt to regain the benevolence of the Venetians after the harsh repressions following the 1848–1849 upheavals, allowed the public to walk along the avenue flanking the San Marco Basin. The result was the need to separate, with a long iron gate, the Garden (reserved for the Royal Court), from the avenue which had now become public.

The gate which since 1816 had limited access from the Ponte della Zecca was therefore repositioned to mark the new entrance to the Gardens: the gateway's monumental features were emphasised by two new stone pillars surmounted by imperial eagles, which were later removed as soon as Venice became part of the Kingdom of Italy. Even the iron and cast-iron pergola, which crosses the garden lengthwise, was then conceived to offer a shaded and private walk, replacing the one that previously consisted of the tree-lined avenue along the Basin. A temporary "covered road," which was built to welcome the sovereigns in November 1856, was adapted for this purpose.

[1] Historical research by Anna Messinis.

The Pavilion by Lorenzo Santi, until that time used in summer by the Royal Court as a relaxation corner and in winter as a greenhouse, was also opened to the public as a coffee house.

Permission for the public use of the avenue, revoked by Empress Sisi in 1861, was re-confirmed by the Savoy family in 1866. Access from the Piazzetta di San Marco to the avenue was bolstered by an iron bridge built over the Rio della Zecca and inaugurated only in 1872, while the garden and the palace remained connected by the drawbridge, rebuilt in 1893 with an iron structure that is still standing.

The use of the garden changed radically after World War I: on 23 December 1920, the Royal Gardens, among the assets ceded by the Crown as state property, were assigned to the Municipality of Venice and made entirely public. The Municipality, while retaining its sinuous layout, made minor changes to the design of the flowerbeds to facilitate the movement of visitors and devised various hypotheses for accessing the garden from St. Mark's Square through the former Royal Palace. They chose the simplest solution, consisting of the passage through the courtyards and over the drawbridge, but experimentation, which began in 1923, was interrupted the following year by Mussolini. Between 1939 and 1940, the design of the garden became geometric again, with extensive use of boxwood and privet, according to the taste of the Fascist regime, which affirmed the primacy of the "Italian garden." The Pavilion by Lorenzo Santi, no longer a *Cafehaus* since the late nineteenth century, had been the headquarters of the Bucintoro Rowing Company for over sixty years, becoming in 1962 the Air Terminal of the new airport, and most recently the information point of the Municipal Tourist Office. In recent decades, the gardens fell into a state of disrepair due to the lack of the necessary upkeep and maintenance. The pergola was in ruins, the drawbridge was unusable, the gate was rusted and crumbling; a reinforced concrete bunker, built during World War II, occupied the central area, and several service buildings erected over the years were in a deplorable state. On 23 December 2014, the State Property Office assigned management of the Royal Gardens to the Venice Gardens Foundation to execute the restoration and take care of them in the years to come.

DUCKS AND MUSIC

PAOLO PEJRONE

in conversation with

LUCA MOLINARI

Luca M. I'd like to start from an interesting point of this story: we began to rethink St. Mark's Square from a garden.

Paolo P. In a certain sense, the garden of Venice was a challenge, since we have given the city and its visitors a public garden, but we treated it as if it were a private one, something that happens very rarely in Italy: designed to accommodate large numbers, but planted and cared for with a botanical and architectural attention usually reserved for an exclusive and protected place.

Paolo P. Even though it might look like an abandoned green area that grows and expands, with plants growing upon each other, it has been treated with almost surgical care. It was certainly a fascinating game, but also an act of faith, because the soil, the location, were by no means easy to work with. I believe that one of the most difficult decisions that needed to be taken and explained to the client was the realism and humility of keeping the strip of land in the sea exactly as it was, without touching or modifying this part of Venice that has remained intact over the last eighty years. There was also a precise and profound determination to keep it after the enormous effort that was put into it, after the difficult and complicated work spent on restoring it. The most heroic act of all, on closer inspection, lies in its excellent daily maintenance.
The result is a garden that arouses curiosity. The people working there have to continuously answer visitors' questions, such as: "What kind of plant is this?", "How is it grown?", "How much does it grow?", as if it were a contemporary surrogate for a botanical garden.

Luca M. Location is a topic that I would like to address in detail later on. Needless to say, this part of the strip of land in the sea protects the garden in some way.

Paolo P. Exactly.

Luca M. When you conducted the inspection, what did you find? In what condition was it?

Paolo P. The situation was terrible, much worse than anyone could have imagined. We showed courage by removing the huge reinforced concrete bunker, symbol of the regime, built to defend St. Mark's bell tower and, above all, the Basilica. We eliminated it and returned that space to the garden.
There were also old plants that had been kept as part of the *status quo* by the previous management: we kept everything we could, removing only what was too shabby or very young, added six years ago by the gardeners and which was mostly inconsistent with the rest.
Generally speaking, except for some sophora, a locust tree, and a hackberry tree, we did not find historical, monumental plants and therefore we chose to highlight the historical nature of architectural forms, such as the pergola, mindful of the Hapsburg cast iron artefacts of the Biedermeier period, which have profoundly influenced the aesthetics of the garden. We recovered the pergola, which was falling apart, and restored it to its former glory.
We also had to consider the greenhouse effect. By adapting to it we were able to include particular plants, that are almost never present in the traditional landscape of Venetian gardens. These are species which, thirty years ago, we could not have planted because the cold weather would have...

Luca M. Killed them.

Paolo P. Wiped them out. We planted about six thousand agapanthuses, without being afraid of aesthetic repetition. The rules of the old Romantic and nineteenth-century garden were adopted, consisting of clusters that create strength, from decisive positions, and we made the garden extremely healthy, lifting up the vegetation so that it would not sink into the mud.
We chose very simple and showy plants, linked in one way or another to the great history of Venice, the Adriatic, Greece, and Turkey. We created a remarkable ensemble, blending many different inspirations, but all held together by the well-known cosmopolitanism of La Serenissima. We tried to keep in mind, also through plants, that Venice is Venice.
The Gardens reflect this melting pot, they are a place blessed by God, which draws together all the charm of the lagoon. I also hoped to be able to introduce some ducks, free to roam the garden, to see them wandering around the canal and the banks. Hopefully in time, we will get there.
The Spring of Arethusa teaches us a lesson here... The decision to place plants in large numbers, acting as eye-catchers, proved decisive and successful. This is perhaps why the garden is so popular.

Luca M. True, it is also very popular with Venetians.

Paolo P. Of course, especially with Venetians, since they have understood its use, they know that it is not some impromptu initiative, it is not a toy. There are people who work there every day, clean it, take care of it, as is the case in any proper garden.
We wanted to include many seats, in this case cast iron and wood benches, to make it a hospitable place to stop and take a rest.
The terracotta pots of Impruneta, perhaps the largest existing in Italy, are intended to be a demonstration to the world of the unrivalled Italian, especially Tuscan, artisan mastery. The vases contain fruit trees, reminiscent of the great gardens of Northern Europe, Germany but also Czechoslovakia. We played with fruit and memories: figs were the glory of the Sanssouci in Potsdam, the pride of Frederick II; pomegranates remind us of Istanbul; the Japanese medlars of a not-so-distant Orient, the bitter oranges (*Citrus x aurantium*) of China and Marco Polo. There is always a bond and there is always a reason.

Luca M. Bringing memories to light is interesting.

Paolo P. Highlighting and explaining it is important. We offer many suggestions, we answer many questions. Above all, as I said, we offer a private garden to the public.

Luca M. It's a unique case.

Paolo P. It's absolutely unique even in Europe.

Luca M. I imagine that working on gardens in Venice is very complicated, because you have to consider the relationship with salt water, with the lagoon.

Paolo P. Salt water, of course, but also supply-related challenges. Making a garden in Venice is complex, there are many variables linked to the specificity of the place and this is why having non-Venetian workers involved is often a mistake.

Luca M. Indeed, perhaps also because the Venetians are highly "protective," so to speak.

Paolo P. The choice of gravel was also interesting. At first, I thought of a material I saw in Portugal, a gravel made of old shells, clam shells. However, we realised that perhaps we were not ready yet for something like that in Italy, so we chose another type of gravel, a gravel from the Brenta River, which has been the only choice that was criticised in our renovation of the garden.

Luca M. Oh, really?

Paolo P. Yes, I received a letter in which it is defined as too light for sunny summer days, because it reflects the light. I think a pair of dark glasses would solve the problem...

Luca M. But the garden is very shady, I saw it in the summer. I would return to the function of the garden, a place which is both public and private. This is the way it evolved. It has always been like that, right?

Paolo P. It was a private garden originally, but before long it was opened to the public.

Luca M. And in the most public area of the city.

Paolo P. Of course, in the most public position of all.

Luca M. What was the garden like originally?

Paolo P. It wasn't there. Or, rather, there were remnants. Strange that no one had thought of taking action before in a place like that, in the centre of the world. Perhaps because setting up a garden is always a debated issue: a work for the common good, a pleasant place for the population, but at the same time often perceived with annoyance, as a place that never ends, changes constantly, requires care as the roots of the trees extend, the leaves fall, and the boughs take away light.

Luca M. The garden is alive.

Paolo P. There is an embryonic love for gardens and plants and at the same time an atavistic mistrust, I would say almost a sort of ill-concealed hatred. Unfortunately, in Italy and abroad, there is a profound ignorance about them.

Luca M. Of course. But it is interesting because you found yourself working on a garden of recent history, totally different from traditional Venetian gardens.

Paolo P. Of course, quite different.

Luca M. It's an imperial form, I would say.

Paolo P. It was a playful garden, an appendage of the Hofburg in Vienna, built with the same methodology, a bit like the Miramare garden, although not of that period.

Luca M. It's an exceptional garden for Venice.

Paolo P. It reminds me so much of another Hapsburg garden, which I find beautiful, in Vallagarina. The Guerrieri Gonzaga park of Villa Lagarina. More than a park it is rather a garden, made up of flower beds and rows, cared for with the attention and precision of an embroiderer.

Luca M. I get what you're saying. One might even say that it's a Biedermeier garden.

Paolo P. The Biedermeier period did not appreciate the large park or the extended horizon. The attention was on the garden, which was contained, extremely well-kept and non-repetitive, rich in episodes, a pond, a small fountain. A brilliant ensemble of many, minute evocations.

Luca M. A Romantic garden.

Paolo P. Yes, Schubert's Romanticism.

Luca M. Exactly. So, this was the idea you started from to conceive the garden as it appears now, endowed with a certain public grace.

Paolo P. Yes, but we were also inspired by the discovery of pergola pieces.

Luca M. Were there any fragments?

Paolo P. Yes, they had fallen into ruins, few were still standing and, luckily, untouched and left in place.

Luca M. Of course. It was abandoned.

Paolo P. Working on this garden had its pros and cons, but collaborating with the architect Torsello was productive.

Luca M. It's true, however, that the garden is now well cared for. The Venetians greatly appreciated this intervention.

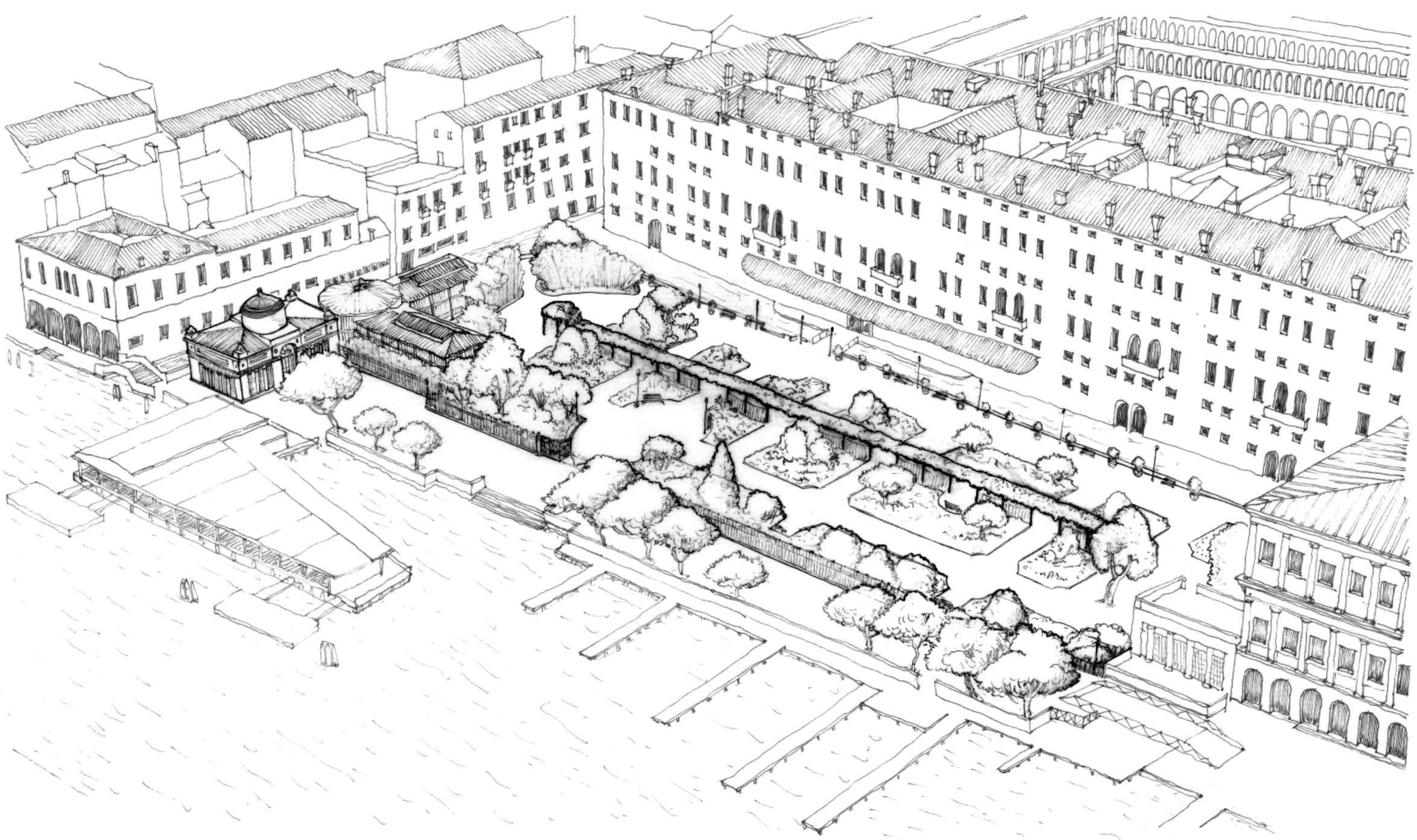

Paolo P. Yes, they did. Also because of the benches that were systematically put in place. To replace the missing or damaged benches, we made copies of an old model found on the spot. The same procedure was used for the pergola. Benches and pergola thus take on a particular meaning, they are the symbol of Italian and Habsburg craftsmanship, bearing witness to the history and culture of an age.

Luca M. Yes, indeed, even the choice of fruit plants, which you told us about, becomes a way to interpret, let's say, the universal, Mediterranean DNA of Venice, which reaches as far as China and then returns to these trees.

Paolo P. Yes, there are several influences in this garden and it would have been a shame to forget them. Placing the fruit trees in terracotta pots first of all allowed us to protect the earth from salt water, and at the same time it gave us the opportunity to show the skill of the potters, to remember the fruits, the links with the different geographical areas and with history.
We also deliberately chose non-native plants for the garden.

Luca M. So, it was a polysemic choice?

Paolo P. Yes, cosmopolitan and polysemic.

Luca M. Cosmopolitan and polysemic, which represents Venice, a melting pot of styles and culture?

Paolo P. Precisely. It's all there.

Luca M. During the works you also had some high water to deal with, am I right?

Paolo P. Yes. We faced all sorts of problems, including the last, devastating, very high water of November 2019. Let's just hope it was the last.

Luca M. Hopefully, the MOSE will keep the situation under control.

Paolo P. However, it went well, but only by a few centimetres.

Luca M. Really? Is the garden in an elevated position? It looks low to me.

Paolo P. We had made contingency plans for flooding, but the garden is positioned a little higher than St. Mark's Square. The base of vases was lapped by salt water, but it was enough to wash them out with fresh water. We were worried about the old trees, but they pulled through.

Luca M. Of course, cleaning with fresh water is essential. And the old trees have already seen so much high water...

Paolo P. Then came the testing, and the grand opening in December 2019. Believe me, I would never have thought we would manage to complete the restoration. It was by no means an easy job. It could have been another broken dream.

Luca M. That's right. Venice often kills its projects.

Paolo P. Collaboration with the Superintendencies was exemplary, they understood the project, supported, and followed through on it.

Luca M. Generali was an important, very generous client.

Paolo P. Yes, they understood the intervention and offered their support.

Luca M. Over the past five years, Generali has operated in St. Mark's Square—between the Procuratie Vecchie and the Royal Gardens—like no other has done in the last three or four hundred years. The first Generali headquarters, two years after opening in Trieste, were in St. Mark's Square. The Procuratie Vecchie have housed their offices for decades. Their support thus becomes a kind of necessary inheritance. Going back to the garden, how can we make it age well? In addition to routine maintenance, what needs to be done?

Paolo P. I'd like it to grow old with a little music every now and then, to host some small concerts.

Luca M. And the ducks you mentioned. Not a bad idea.

Paolo P. Ducks and music.

Luca M. It would be great, like going back to the nineteenth century.

Paolo P. In this regard, I would like to point out that the neoclassical pavilion also comes to life with the opening of the cafeteria.

Luca M. I'd like to ask you one last question. During your career you have dealt with many historic gardens, taking action in very different situations, so was Venice a special project?

Paolo P. It was absolutely unique and not a repeat of other gardens. It's the first private public garden. I wanted to create a monument to the garden, not to the author, not to the place. The collaboration with Generali generated respect for the place, and we made it contemporary without distorting it, and without forcing it. My philosophy is that you don't necessarily have to surprise.
To create a garden, there is no need to erect a green wall or vertical woods, it's not necessary to use artifices or place plants, deprived of their ability to communicate, in difficult-to-grow contexts for the sole purpose of glorifying someone's ingenuity.

Luca M. Your work is discreet.

Paolo P. My work was based on discretion and reality, which is always the fruit of knowledge. It's essential to have maximum confidence in plants, to understand their development, growth and needs. In public gardens, trees are often arranged in close proximity to one other, too close, to immediately create a finished effect that satisfies the eye of the visitor and, above all, of the administration. Popular decisions, extremely easy to understand, which then require drastic and continuous pruning and in the long run form the habit of considering these schematic solutions as the norm. The garden does not exist unless I cut, trim, crush, or mutilate it. And even in the case of well-executed pruning—we may happen to see, for example, a row of beautifully cut plane trees—and one wonders if it was really necessary. Letting a tree grow as freely as possible, when the conditions are right, is not part of our gardening culture. Instead, there seems to be a sort of instinct to own the existence of the plant to affirm our own being and to exorcise our fears... In the Venice garden we tried to counteract this vision: the garden is a garden, and in order to grow luxuriant it must be taken care of and maintained, but not vexed. This is not a matter of strength dynamics, but of cohabitation and natural growth.

Luca M. How do you place the Royal Gardens of Venice in your line of work?

Paolo P. I am satisfied with the work done and it embodies a great deal of my "botanical" love. Overall, the outcome is positive.

Luca M. And what kinds of love were satisfied in this garden?

Paolo P. The greatest one is agapanthus, which I have passionately loved for sixty years. I thought it was very rare, because we hardly ever saw it, I used to find it only in some Tuscan or Roman gardens, and then I thought that, coming from South Africa, I would never be able to plant it in the north.
It is always necessary to consider the exact origin of a plant when bringing it into a garden, in order for it to acclimatise successfully. For example, the vegetation of equatorial Africa should be distinguished from that of the Atlas Mountains in Morocco.

Luca M. Of course, selecting the right plant for the context is important.

Paolo P. Agapanthus has some huge advantages: a beautiful winter foliage, thrives for nine months, with a robust colour, and a long summer flowering of about twenty days. I then introduced, to uphold the Italian nature of the place, the mastic, the myrtle, and the "Contessa Sara" *Bignonia Ricasoliana* which has a peculiar history: it is an "Italian" plant even though it originates from the Transkei in South Africa, because it was planted for the first time in the small botanical garden of the Ricasoli family on the banks of Porto Ercole in Tuscany, in the Grosseto area. This beautiful evergreen plant, with a long flowering in September, has become the leitmotif of the pergola. And then I added plenty of jasmine. Many fragrant plants. I would have liked to include the great Chilean rhubarb, but the conditions were not suitable. So, I replaced it, and to create some amazement, I placed the large leaves of the Chinese rice paper plant in the centre of the garden, which look almost bulky, but respect the effect required by the botanical art of the past, when, next to potted plants placed in greenhouses and flower beds, there was always a high-impact area where the tallest lilies and the most broad-leaved shrubs were placed.

Luca M. It's a beautiful plant that takes us back to the cosmopolitan essence of Venice, to its relations with China, to the Silk Road, and to Marco Polo.

– FROM HISTORY TO GLOBAL IMPACT –

ACQUA ALTA

GUADALUPE NETTEL

Amongst the numerous islands that surround the city of Venice, there are three particularly sombre ones: San Michele, a beautiful cemetery full of trees; San Servolo, which for decades was home to a psychiatric hospital, and San Lazzaro, an old leper colony. The three represent the states that regularly cut humans off from society. One only has to visit these islands to imagine how the world was a few years ago. Quite different in appearance, but similar in terms of relations.

Many years ago, in the 1910s, a man arrived at San Servolo. It wasn't that he decided to move there; he had in fact been forced to do so, as almost always happens in such cases: we social beings make sure that there is always someone who occupies the "outside," whether they be from another country, of another colour, or someone with more delicate health or a more sensitive personality than ours, in order to feel that, unlike them, we form part of the group. They selected him when he was just a young man. Some say it was bad luck, others that it was deliberate, as he used to quake at loud noises, cry for reasons that to everyone else seemed absurd, and hardly slept because he spent his nights listening to the frenzied chatter of the seagulls.

One morning they came looking for him at the bakery on Riva de l'Ogio where he'd worked for nearly two years. The owner wasn't there that day, having gone out to deliver a cake for a wedding banquet in Mestre, on the outskirts of the city. The men asked him if he was Alessio Favaro, and he tried hard to reply as honestly as he could: "Sometimes I am," he told them. "Sometimes I'm just the baker."

The two men exchanged a conspiratorial glance, which he had seen before in the eyes of people prepared to do him harm, and they resolved to take him with them. They took hold of him, one on each side, and crossed his arms inside a misshapen shirt. To him a shirt had always been a sign of respect, a symbol of belonging. He put one on to go to church, for instance, or to accompany someone who was on their way to the cemetery. Except this wasn't a soft, neatly ironed shirt like the one he wore on important days. This shirt would not have looked good on anyone. It was one of those garments that made one feel different and maladjusted just by wearing it, as if one had donned a costume and a Mattaccino mask during lent. This shirt had sleeves so long they hung down way below the wearer's hands, making whoever wore it look like a simpleton, or a child dressing up in his father's clothes. As Alessio was so young, anyone who came and peered in through the window would have thought just this—that inside was a kid playing at dressing up, above all because he was still trying to be nice and was smiling at the men politely, wondering if perhaps, after agreeing to try on this strange item of clothing, he could sell them a cake, or at least a focaccia.

But the men were not customers, not even potential ones. Once Alessio put his arms inside the shirt, they tied the sleeves together behind his back and began pushing him much like the way the boys at school had done when, at his father's insistence, he had attended primary for a few years. Alessio became upset and he too hit out at the men who were hassling him, at first gently, then as fiercely as he could. One of them took out a notebook and wrote down two words. Alessio tried to read them but, though he recognised all the letters, he couldn't grasp the meaning. They were closed words, monolithic as a pair of prison cells. His heart was beating very fast and across his face he felt a heat spread, much like when he stepped too close to the oven. The men continued to push, and eventually got him out of the building and took him down the street, despite his struggles to free himself and the cries for help he uttered. They made him walk past the fish market, in full view of everyone, but nobody came out to defend him, even though he was known by many there. They knew his brothers and sisters, and his parents, and were generally friendly towards him. That morning, however, not one person said a word to him. They looked down at the ground or turned their heads away. At most, when they heard him call their names, they threw him a pitying smile. On more than one occasion he heard them murmuring the names of Lucia and of Signor Scarpa, her husband. Little by little, the rage he felt disappeared, giving way to humiliation, and the weight of this familiar feeling made him walk meekly, followed by his captors along the narrow streets of the Sestiere di San Marco towards the main square, where he had seen Lucia for the last time. It had been a Sunday, his day off, and as such his clothes were not dusted with flour or chocolate. He had entered the Basilica for a few minutes to sit down in a pew. He liked to savour the atmosphere that still hung in the church after mass. The smell of damp and incense impregnated the air in the same way the aroma of bread wafted out of the bakery and along Riva de l'Ogio, drawing people in. Alessio stayed there a few minutes and, when he began to grow bored, he walked out slowly, imitating the deliberate, respectful footsteps of the parishioners. It was then that he saw her. She was outside, hidden behind one of the wooden doors, dressed in blue. Elegant and lovely, as ever. Lucia was the younger sister of Pietro, the ice-cream seller. They had played together every day as children until her parents married her off. Since then, they saw each other less, and always in secret. It was said that Signor Scarpa was an ill-tempered man, and much older than she, though Alessio had never seen him. When he saw Lucia behind the door of the church, he smiled in surprise. She took him by the hand, leading him zig-zagging through the columns of the Palazzo Ducale to another hiding place in a shadowy corner. He recalled precisely the temperature of Lucia, warm as a balm on that February afternoon. He also recalled that a man passed by very close to where they were, calling her insistently. Alessio tried to tell her it was time to go: the tide was rising, and the square would soon be flooded, but no sooner had he opened his mouth than the girl placed the palm of her hand over it. She was so close to him he could hear the ragged pace of her breathing. The boy's eyes slid down helplessly towards the girl's breasts just before him, and this is how he came to see the marks from some enormous fingers on her neck. The man walked past again shouting angrily, closer this time. Alessio felt his gaze gleaming like the eyes of a predator in the depths of a forest, and felt afraid of what he might do to him. Then he too began to run through the alleyways. This time the girl didn't stop him. That night, the slaves of the Orologio rang the bells with uncommon fury and the gulls screeched nothing but dire omens.

On Tuesday at noon, two men dragged Alessio through St. Mark's Square towards the Bacino. They did not queue up to board the vaporetto, the only boat he had ever used to get across to the islands, but instead took their own means of transport, a white vessel like the ambulances that sometimes sped along the canals, forcing the gondoliers to move out of the way. A few feet away a funeral barge was sailing towards San Michele. On board, dressed head to toe in black, was the ice-cream seller Pietro's family. The men untied the boat and pushed off into the water without explaining to Alessio where they were taking him, but by this point, nothing they might say to him could have mattered less.

RETHINKING ST. MARK'S SQUARE

MICHEL LUSSAULT and ITAI PALTI

in conversation with

LUCA MOLINARI

Luca M. The focus of our conversation today is St. Mark's Square, which is, as Michel would say, a *hyper-lieu*. It's an incredibly traditionalist, iconic place, but it's also a place of consumption, of tourism. This piazza has a powerful symbolic value. I would like to start from this basic element: St. Mark's Square as an icon, a global image, and simultaneously a specific place. I would like to start right away with your reflections about the perception of St. Mark's Square, your experience and your considerations about this place.

Itai P.. I see three important facets: the symbolic meaning of St. Mark's Square, the dialogical role of the space, and the experiential one.
Let's focus on the symbolic meaning first. This square is certainly a statement that some might define violent. I would rather say it is imposing.
It is a very structured space in which the visitor becomes an object dwarfed and surrounded by aesthetics of power. The square's interior, is defined by three rigid facades encompassing a flat, inhabitable plane that makes one feel exposed. Habitable spaces are only afforded by the colonnades of the "hosting" structures, a further representation of ownership.
What intent is embedded in this space? Is it really a public space that symbolises the pride of Venetians, or has its preservation frozen its symbolic meaning as an outdated display of authority?
Look at the bodies housed in these buildings. We know that historically they served those who wielded power over the public, and the square is designed to enforce, almost cement, this dynamic. This is a dynamic we must question. Can we flip the square so that the public may feel it is there to serve them?

Luca M. It's interesting because, as you know, the specific case of St. Mark's Square shows a clear relationship between architecture and symbols. Each building is a perfect representation of parts of the system of the Venetian Republic, where every building embodied something. There's the Marciana Library which represents knowledge, there was the barn representing wealth, there is the St. Mark's Basilica, which represents sacredness, Palazzo Ducale, and the symbolism of Saint Mark and Saint George, a clock tower, symbol of time and production, and then the arches, somehow representing the idea of community in a markedly orthogonal and perspective manner. It was the representation of a specific government, but since Venice was an authentic Republic, it was also the representation of a large community. And we must not forget that St. Mark's Square was also designed to be seen arriving from the sea. So, there was also the perception of the people coming from the sea and immediately seeing the symbol of Venice when coming from the East. Now we are living in a completely different time. All that symbolism may not be understood by common people and tourists. We would like to know from Michel—considering his definition of space—what he thinks about what Itai said, also in relation to defining St. Mark's Square a *hyper-lieu*.

> St. Mark's Square shows a clear relationship between architecture and symbols. Each building is a perfect representation of parts of the system of the Venetian Republic.

Michel L. I may perhaps surprise you but I do not approach St. Mark's as a Venetian or Italian square, but as a square that "belongs" to all inhabitants of the world, or at least one that can be shared. Not only because of tourism, but also because of the power of the "geographical imagination" that emanates from it. St. Mark's Square is iconic, in the sense that it is known and recognised by most people, including those who will never visit it, but who can dream about it.
In a sense St. Mark's Square is a kind of global common, resisting privatisation by economic actors. Even if you are a tourist for one day, when you walk through this square you take possession, for a moment, of this common good. I always have a very strange feeling when I observe St. Mark's, because privatisation is everywhere obviously, but at the same time it's also obvious that St. Mark's is a kind of common spatial good.

Luca M. I agree. This connects us to the idea of fluidity in the use of what we call a square. In the previous centuries, squares were designed with a specific ideological and political vision.
The space exists but the people use it in a completely different way.
We'd like to discuss with you how an historical icon and perfectly designed space can be lived by different and fluid communities in the present time.

Michel L. "Communalisation," the construction of the piazza as a global, common space, shared by the practices of "habitation" of individuals who occupy the square, whatever the reason and the duration for this "inhabitation" may be, is linked to the development of tourism. The "touristification" of the world is the vector, the driver of the communalisation of the square. If I wanted to be a little ironic, I could say that if tourism stopped, St. Mark's Square would not be able to be a common spatial good at all. If we want St. Mark's to be a common good, tourism must be efficient, it must work. It's a strange situation because very often, people emphasise the fact that tourism is destroying St. Mark's, but from a certain point of view, it is the opposite. Without tourism and tourists, the square immediately deflates and that's exactly what we have been seeing since March 2020 with lockdown. The end of touristic activities put the square's capability of being a common good on hold.
I would add a second point. I am always fascinated when I observe how people use "selfies," in order both to privatise and publicise the square and most of all how they use the square, the way they inhabit it. When you take a photo of yourself within a place, you privatise it, because you make it your own, but also, if you share the photographs on Instagram, Tik Tok, Facebook etc., you publicise the square and your experience of it. To me, a hyper-place (*hyper-lieu*) is exactly the kind of space where everything is ambiguous; any social practice is a matter of very subtle relationships between communalisation, publicising, privatisation, effect of powers, effect of liberty etc.

Luca M. Itai, what do you think about this paradox, so to speak, that Michel introduced? It's very provocative and it is also a theoretical paradox, which I think is very interesting. Being private and being public to common communities and communal things.
But who cares about any this, since people just walk across the space? What is the role of design and of practice in working with this kind of social and cultural interactions?

Itai P. I think this is a political question hinged on whether or not a space should be exploited for an abstract value. This notion of a space being commodified by people who barely set foot in it, to me is worrisome, although very common. As much as we may enjoy consuming the symbolic meaning of such spaces, I feel that it is a privilege we should question. To me it is a form of exploitation, a draining of a space that should serve the people who inhabit it rather than the fleeting visitors.
This form of exploitation is something I think we can link well to the effects of tourism on Venice. The commodification of the square by the rest of the world prevents the space from becoming localised. Its freezing into a museum deprives it of that very important ability of public space to absorb memory, and to create dialogue. These things disappear in order to avoid disruption of its symbolism. And, maybe because of my own ideals, I believe that St. Mark's Square would be better if it were less symbolic and became a more living, breathing, dynamic space.
Tourism has sanitised Venice; the locals are living in a museum curated for the rest of the world and not a space serving local lives, well-being, and aspirations. The nature of this tourism should be challenged, because it's an unhealthy addiction. Venice has to strike a healthier balance in order to sustain itself. It has to be a living city, as well as one that people can visit.

Luca M. I was thinking that, since the Renaissance, Venice has always been a place of tourism. Wealthy visitors would go back home with Canaletto paintings as postcards. Mine is a provocation, but it is to say that Venice has been considered a global symbolic form for centuries, not only nowadays. But there was a balance because the community of Venetian people was larger, it was a city of a hundred thousand people. But now the point is that that balance has been completely lost, because the community of Venetians is growing smaller and the city has been in a way worn out in terms of local community in favour of a fluid, larger, community coming from outside. It's a kind of unbalance causing what you say, isn't it? But for us Venetians, what we have been experiencing in recent years, is that there are new institutions and foundations that come to the city to transform old buildings into new public spaces, giving rise to new kinds of communities. It's not only globalisation in terms of consumption, but globalisation in terms of considering Venice a new hub where you can stay and deliver new kinds of knowledge, which brings us back to new communities. Regeneration, and political and economic repurposing become spatial variations, which allow new communities to use the same city in a completely different way.

Itai P. I think this is a very good point you make. Venice through the centuries has been a place of dialogue for the rest of the world. It's therefore worth asking whether the state of its main public square is representative of that dialogue or not.

To me it's a matter of what forms of expression you give to the people who are in a space. You mention selfies as a way of "personalising" the space, for example. To me this is a very limited scope for expression, almost like museum rules. If we are saying the importance of Venice resides in dialogue, then dialogue must be the priority in designing the city.

Michel L. I must say that, to me, throughout its history Venice has rarely been only a local city, but rather the stage of a great power and a place from where the city tried to rule all the Mediterranean Sea and the entire European world. Venice is a very specific configuration of space, economic activities, and power. And its urban patterns and architectures express that Venice is in fact more a realm than a city. Thus, it's not surprising that today the entire contemporary global world is encapsulated in St. Mark's Square. It is only logical that in St. Mark's we find the expression of the strengths and weaknesses of our contemporary world. The world manifests itself, for better or for worse, through the organisation of this square, its functioning, and the practices of the different social actors who occupy it and make it live.

That's the reason why to me Itai, it's very difficult to conceive how only people with real citizenship of Venice could live and experience the square, because Venice has never belonged only to Venetian inhabitants and citizens. I have worked extensively with Hannah Arendt because I find in her texts the groundings of my theoretical framework. If I were to summarise it, I would say that space is not something to be owned but something to be shared. What is really important to me is the "shareness," the capability and the will human beings have to share living spaces and therefore organise a political society (Arendt thinks of politics as the specific treatment by human societies of the "space-in-between individuals"), even though they are legal owners of the space. Thus, the reclamation by Venetian citizens to be the unique and exclusive "real" owners of the city is a kind of privatisation.

From this perspective, the relevant question is not how Venetian citizens may become more present in Venice, but rather how the space of St. Mark's Square may be ethically shared by all the human beings who happen to be in this space, for whatever reason, whatever their social status. I think that if we try to understand human spaces as shareable goods, we may also define another way of thinking about the world, and how we could "design" and promote a more equitable and fair

Michel L. world. I think that one of the major issues we must tackle is an excess of ownership. We have too many owners of space, too many claims for exclusivity in the use of social space, which should on the contrary be socialised and shared more.
That's the reason why tourism fascinates me. Of course, contemporary tourism shows many questionable and excessive aspects. But the fact remains that tourists inhabit the world and tend to make it a common and shareable "glocal" (a mix of global and local) space. So the question that arises is not how to banish tourists from "my" place, but rather how to promote ethical and fair tourism and make tourism an instrument for thoughts and actions towards the sharing of spatial goods. I think it's not only an abstract question, it's not only a rhetorical assumption, but also a very pragmatical one, especially in the case of Venice and St. Mark's Square.

Luca M. Clearly we must consider all elements: sharing, caring and design. Because, sharing is the natural effort of our community to consider cities as welcoming places. A place where you share not only what you see, but also yourself, and you take care of it, of course. Taking care of a city means being aware of it And in the meantime, I rely on sharing based on good design, because good design can't be only about design of a new square or a new floor. Design is also about a hypothesis, about a modality of relationship, and more. You know this very well because this is what you do. So, how do you feel about the relationship between these three words: sharing, caring and design?

Itai P. When we talk about, for example, the tradition of Venice sharing its spaces with the rest of the world, there are foundational questions to be asked.
Are we required to honour and perpetuate this tradition?
Is this still what we want?
We can celebrate Venice as a shared space where an international dialogue occurred, but today's tourism is different. In the past, people didn't come

Itai P. to Venice just to see the place. They came to do something and make something of themselves, to learn, to commit, to evolve. And that's very different from today's tourism that's about arriving, consuming, and leaving. This is where caring and design come into play. Design is our opportunity to infuse a space with intent. The intent to recognise, empathise, and give agency to different people in a space to generate connections. We should ask ourselves if we could return to a healthier balance for Venice, one that may contribute to the city's growth and evolution. Can we bring up ideas? Can we have this kind of conversation? Can we bring something with us and change the process? This would be a real dialogue introducing caring via design. The city caring for the people, and in return the people caring for the city, creating a symbiosis.

Michel L. This is interesting, Itai. I will add a nuance, regarding design and its capacity to propose a "caring city," a concept that I sometimes find hard to understand. For me, what we share when we walk through St. Mark's Square is not so much the space itself (the architectural and urban form) but rather the experience of this space and the relationship with the other humans "embarking" with us at the same time into the practice of that place.
To share space is in fact to share an experience of spatiality which imposes to stabilise relations of good distance with the other humans, with the non-humans (think of the role of the pigeons in St. Mark's Square), and with the physical elements of the space. Spatiality is this unique experience of "betweenness" and regulation of placement and distance. And if you look at the experience of tourists in the square, you will observe that people are sharing the betweenness.
Any space of practice is imposed, compulsory; one does not invent it as an individual. But the experience of spatiality, the experience of the "in-between," is one much less imposed.
Of course one acts according to rules and competences of spatiality (and the tourist practice is very much regulated by geographical imaginations that define what one may or may not do, what one must and must not do), but there are also plenty of possibilities to play with the rules. Through practice, one invents one's daily life, as Michel de Certeau wrote. Spatiality is an adventure, a composition in a situation of distance and location relations with other human and non-human agencies, as well as with the "framework" of the pre-existing built space.
Thus, caring for me is not so much about taking care of space rather of spatiality.

Itai P. These are reflections of political values, and there are a couple of issues here which I think differently about. Firstly, I think every city can be a caring city, that every city should be a caring city, and that this means giving up some things we've grown used to. I'm ok with giving up what Venice means to me, as an outsider, if it creates a more caring city for its people. I think the world would be a better place if we thought more like this. You're right, every built environment is an imposition, but the question is who is imposing, who they are imposing on, and whether there is exploitation or not.
In my opinion, we need to be less sentimental about what Venice means to us as outsiders, and more equitable in what it means for those living in it. And yes, that means also giving up some romanticised qualities but I think that's the nature of pushing for "the right to the city." It is a right to "reshape ourselves by reshaping the city," asking what kind of society we want to be and designing the city according to those values.

Luca M. It's very difficult to make these considerations in relation to a place that is so fully crystallised. Furthermore, we do not consider St. Mark's Square only as a square. It's true that sometimes it can be considered as a sought-after place, but things are far more complex. St. Mark's is at the core of a ramification of a public space that is far more complex, that redefines the space of the city as a unique space, because in a way, in Venice, what people have always been most impressed by in Venice, is its powerful human dimension. I mean, you feel it, in a good way, because there are no cars, spaces are of completely different sizes and so, in a way, sometimes stepping into St. Mark's Square is part of an experience of a much more complex urban system. We should not focus on the idea of the square as a kind of autonomous space, independent from a more branched out urban structure. A way to bring new life into a place like St. Mark's Square would be to use the entire city in a different way, to work on the city and not on St. Mark's where you can't pull down buildings. You can work in different ways on the city, with practices that would allow a completely different way of living the square, don't you think? It's something less tangible but more effective.

But at the same time, the city is always a form of dialogue between its image and its continuous changes. I mean, if you look at the city itself, St. Mark's Square is changing: for instance, the Procuratie Vecchie that David Chipperfield is working on, will transform the square as never before.

And internally the city is continuously changing. So, there is an image of the city from the outside, with shops changing continuously, and all the people moving. The urban ecology is far more complex. The city dies, lives, and revives every day. And the way we use it, the way we experience it, and the project we have for the city, for the next decades are so important. I think that probably the way we work on a city like Venice may become a template urban project for the years to come.

Michel L. As I said before, I try to define what I call spatial care as an attention to spatiality. The question I ask myself is: how can we be fairer, attentive, ethical in our spatial relationship with others who share, through their practices, a "moment of space" with us? This is what we share: the experience of a "moment of space in common."

If we accept this theoretical proposition, would it be possible, in Venice and elsewhere, to think about a relationship with tourism that would show more care both from the tourists to the other "actors" (e.g. agencies or stake holders) of this moment of place, and from the "actors" to the tourists? And what kind of "design" should we invent for this, which would not be a formal design of space, but a political and ethical design of spatiality? That's my first question.

I also have a second one, more related to the political issue you brought up: what kind of global societies do we want to construct on a global world scale? Could we construct a caring world? A caring global world? Do we have the capability to share common moments of space and experience spatiality on a global world scale? And, if we want to promote inclusive societies, since sharing and caring cannot be only addressed to locals, but also to foreigners, tourists, strangers, refugees, and migrants, how can we care for, especially for, foreigners, tourists, strangers, migrants and refugees? I believe we must think in terms of a more global picture. Can we invent a world-scale global (urban) society of care?

Itai P. Good questions. I think I touched on the topic of care of tourism, when we spoke about the symbolic meaning of Venice as a place to co-create, learn, and explore. It's absolutely possible to create caring tourism; it's a matter of policy and cultivating that culture. We have good examples already; the Erasmus programme, in my opinion is a caring tourism because it allows a connection to the place, and not just on an emotional level, but also on a biological level. You know, we perceive ourselves as very abstract beings that have abstract connections to places. But when we look at the neurobiological level, then we understand that place is paramount in our cognition and meta-cognition. We map out our memories onto space, and we also recall those memories when we continue to interact with that space. What science teaches me is that we are far less abstract than we think we are. We need connection to a place in order to feel continuity, in order to create a sense of identity, in order to care about that place and about the people in that place.

We need connection to a place in order to feel continuity, in order to create a sense of identity, in order to care about that place and about the people in that place.

Luca M. In the last year, we experienced an important dematerialisation of our physicality. The pandemic has shaped our way of thinking and also our attitude towards the idea of space. It's very interesting how fear somehow shapes spaces. We all experienced how houses can become a lockdown, places where we can be locked in. Being locked down inside our homes, we discovered the importance of the city, but in the meantime, working in the city, we discovered that we also feared the city, because there is something visible that can be seen. So, there is a very interesting connection to what we have been experiencing in the last months...

Itai P. Yes, I don't think we know what we are experiencing.
The pandemic may have sped up a few processes that we still don't fully understand, like the normalisation of digital interactions.
How do they compare to in-person interactions?
My worry is that since empathy is based on how we observe and communicate with people, down to tiny nuances, this incredibly rich experience cannot happen in digital spaces. It's not that we don't empathise online, but it's a "digital empathy." And so, we don't yet understand how this is impacting on our social connections, and our sense of identity.
Therefore, if you want to talk about caring on a global scale, I think there are a lot of hurdles. We want it but I'm not sure that our biology and cognition supports it. That is why creating cities with shared spaces that support genuine connection may be even more paramount in the future.
In my opinion, the less we think about space in abstract terms and the more situated we consider it, the more likely we are to create caring cities.

Michel L. I totally agree with you: the sharing of space cannot happen only via a remote device in a digital space. We have to physically share a space with others in order to be empathic with them. That's the reason why, it's really necessary to promote a global world of motions, of mobility, a global world of exchange, a global world of tourism in a sense, because, when you are a tourist in motion, you are able to physically meet other people, people who are different from you. I know perfectly well that tourism is also a problem, because of the way contemporary tourism is organised, as a globalised industry. But for any individual, tourism is also an experience, an anthropological and spatial one.

The sharing of space cannot happen only via a remote device in a digital space. We have to physically share a space with others in order to be empathic with them.

And, if I may, I have to say that you overestimate the importance of the touristic experience, as an immediate one. The very first moment I am entering in a square, like St. Mark's Square, even though I don't know anything about the square, the very first seconds I'm entering this square and walking across the piazza, I'm experiencing it. I am experiencing it through my body, my senses, I mobilise all my spatial competences to adjust my distance from others, the speed of my step, and to choose a good location for myself. This is done in real time, because our "spatial habitus" is very constituted, structured and internalised. And in a few seconds, this kind of experience can change me, and I can share it with others. We do not experience time in the same way. To a certain extent, we only have a very poor grasp of the passage of time, it is abstract, whereas the experience of space is constant, concrete, without delay. And it feeds us every day, contributing to make each one of us a "spatial actor."

Itai P. Yes, I like how you speak about space! In a way it sounds like we are diverging, but I think we are really converging. I think space is our first language. The very first language that we learned from our social surroundings. And just like every language, there is a grammar, there is structure, and there is syntax. The way that we shape the environment creates the structure of the language, it influences the way we express ourselves, communicate with others, and share experiences. I can walk, I can jump, I can speak or not speak to others, I can protest, I can sing, these are parts of social contracts embedded into the spaces we create.
So what is the level of impact of a space? It is hard to measure sometimes because of the complexity of human experience, especially long-term. But with all this complexity, we are still picking and choosing some significant ingredients.
So what language does St. Mark's Square afford people to speak? I believe there is a conceptual trap here: we think that empty space is a canvas for expression, right? We think that a void allows for all eventualities, but that's not the way expression works. Expression is built on top of grammar and syntax in the way that I just spoke about. So since St. Mark's Square is an empty space, it supports very limited forms of expression.
How can we create a space that affords more?

Michel L. An empty square is also a kind of stage. The famous theatre director Peter Brook, says that every empty space could be a stage. A stage where players can perform. St. Mark's Square could be seen as a stage, where any human being crossing that stage, sitting on that stage, could perform. And I'm very interested in the way geography could deal with theatre and with performance, because, to me, as a geographer, I am more and more looking at empty spaces as stages where individuals have the capability to perform, to perform something for themselves, or/and for the others. When I perform something, I am beginning to share the experience of space. It's a matter of design. And it's also a matter of spatial semantics and grammar. I totally agree with you on one point: tourism is a really poor activity both in terms of semantics and in terms of syntax. What we need to conceive, is a richer spatial semantics and syntax for the tourism of tomorrow.

St. Mark's Square could be seen as a stage, where any human being crossing that stage, sitting on that stage, could perform.

Itai P. Indeed! First of all, I think that in any city it is important to have a void, mostly because it allows the voicing of a collective message. But there are many other square typologies we can look at. Washington Square Park in New York, for example, has plenty of different types of spaces that allow for a rich variety of interactions. So if I'm visiting New York, I go to this square to feel the life of the city, it creates a connection to the place.
Perhaps as part of this aspiration to create a caring tourism that is exemplified by dialogue, we can ask: how much void should be kept? And how much can we give up to allow a richer dialogue? It never needs to be one or the other. You place ingredients and you keep on tasting. Does it work better this way or that way? You have to constantly be questioning the balance of flavours. As it is now, St. Mark's Square is imbalanced, and we are too scared to experiment. But if the place stops being responsive, alive, conscious… it becomes devoid of real life and disassociates from what is relatable.

Michel L. I like what you say about voids in cities. Cities need emptiness, need voids. And I have a really hard time understanding why and how contemporary urban planning, urbanism and architecture have destroyed emptiness and voids in cities.

Itai P. They don't create profit.

Michel L. Exactly, they don't. In Venice, perhaps, it's specific, because there is no emptiness. There is only one void, which is St. Mark's Square: the single "large" open space one can deal with when in Venice. And it's rather different elsewhere. I think we have to look at each city with the will to understand its specificity. Cities all around the world are generic, due to planetary urbanisation, but we must keep in mind that any city is also a specific one. As a geographer I always try to identify the specificity of a given city.

Itai P. Travelling, I have found it very difficult to point out the specificity of many cities. Globalisation and capitalism have flattened out our cities into a generic typology. Venice however is so different; it's very privileged to have this specificity. And of course we don't want to ruin that, but perhaps there is a way to amplify it, to continue its spirit.
Venice did not become Venice by being static. It became this unique place by being innovative, by drawing in and supporting creative energy. It's a question that all historical cities face: can you keep on living if what you are doing is preserving?

Luca M. This is particularly interesting because it is actually a matter of advancing and finding a way of preserving our memory, and at the same time, being open to our future and to the people coming to Venice. What Michel said before is, in my opinion, particularly striking because he asks: can Venice be welcoming to people coming from outside? Are we still able to do this? And I think the answer is that we are able to do it, as long as we keep on working on ourselves, as citizens, as people of the city, and not only, as Michel said, as owners, but as living people, working people, moving people. I think the key is interaction, as you both said.

Itai P. I think living is being curious about the world.
The challenge of built form is that it's often an answer because it has to exist decisively, concretely. But answers are the death of curiosity. We live within questions, therefore we have to keep on challenging the answers that are built around us.
That's living.

Michel L. I realise, Itai, that our difference is that I am less and less interested in material space and its organisation and more and more focused on human spatiality, on the experience of space and its sharing.
Where I agree with you is the idea that the built environment is often conceived and designed to frame spatiality, even control it.
But individuals are very often capable of subverting frameworks, rules, norms, obligations. Spatiality is an art of detour, of going beyond the margins, of freedom, of escape. And even day-trippers, who visit Venice on the run, can escape from the rules for a moment and find a space of freedom, of improvisation.

Itai P. I hear an echo of Bernard Tschumi in these thoughts, someone who influenced my thinking too. You're talking about the duty of someone to enact an environment. Right?
At the beginning of this conversation I also mentioned violence in architecture. I agree with you that people can change the way spaces are used, but I think there is a physical materiality, that most of the time represents a much stronger force. So, I'm questioning the need to be so forceful in architecture. I wonder whether we should allow more of what you're talking about: the reinvention of how people use and therefore reinterpret space.

Michel L. Yes, I totally agree with that.

Itai P. And it's all about the dialogue that you allow.

Michel L. I think you would agree with me if I said that the issue of the linkage between space, the building environment which frames our experiences, and spatiality, the way we perform in space, is perhaps the most important issue we must tackle. It's a political issue, it's an ethical one.
It's also a very important challenge in terms of architecture, design, and conception of space.

Itai P. I frequently reflect on this topic, what I call spatial meta-cognition, our ability to know how we can use space and how it affects us.
For me, that is the ultimate aim of a space, to increase this awareness, this consciousness... it's a magical turning point when space becomes emancipating. Emancipating people from the violence of architecture, by showing them there are other ways of being.

Michel L. Another way to go about this could be education.

Itai P. This is education.

Michel L. To give people the capability to be more and more aware of this metacognition and to be more and more capable of implementing new ways of acting, new ways of thinking spaces, is obviously a matter of education. And what is really interesting to me is to think about the way some kind of public spaces could be considered as "learning spaces." Spaces where one can perform and which give us the capability to "learn" something.

Itai P. To me, if a public space supports learning through play, which is what we're talking about, that is the greatest contribution a space can afford to communities and to visitors, and so on. I absolutely agree with you on that. We can allow people to play and explore. I think it's a very good way forward.

Michel L. I agree. This is a good word to close our conversation.

SUSTAINABILITY BETWEEN LOCAL AND GLOBAL ISSUES

RENATA CODELLO and CESARE BENELLI

in conversation with

DAVIDE RAMPELLO

Davide R. As you may know, Generali has decided to publish a book to recount the whole project of the restoration of the Procuratie Vecchie and the Royal Gardens of Venice. The book will cover many aspects, the history of the square and describe its refurbishment but, ultimately, I have been asked to reflect on Venice, on what Venice is today, and above all on what Venice can represent.

Davide R. Reflections that ultimately stem from the metaphor of "restoration": when you restore a building this action is underpinned by a specific logic, either to give the building a second function, or to validate what it once used to be.
I replied I wished to speak about Venetian culture in a broad sense, with two very close friends. This is a fundamental aspect, because in order for people to gain mutual understanding you need a sincere and strong relationship, based on feelings and affection. The mind "lies," as you say, but when there is a close connection, one where the "heart" and feelings are involved, that's when a good dialogue can grow.

The city cannot be beautiful without the people who made it, the city would otherwise become a beautiful empty shell.

That's why I chose two broad topics that represent the soul of Venice, so to speak: the spirit of hospitality and the spirit of study and research, with all that ensues. This is obviously just a statement that encapsulates a world of specific know-how and knowledge.
So, Renata, there's always much talk about Venice, but first come the people who made it, then come the things they created.
If this city, this extraordinary work of art, is not renewed and redesigned by somebody who is aware of its cultural and artistic history then clearly something is not working. The city cannot be beautiful without the people who made it, the city would otherwise become a beautiful empty shell, like those hermit crabs use as their homes.
I would like Renata to start from this concept, from this narrative, from the origins of the city of Venice and its meanings.

Renata C. In my opinion, one of the fundamental themes regarding Venice is envisioning it as a sustainable city, characterised by water, that is both its friend and foe, by land and the absence of land, and by the salubrity of the area, an aspect that has always been an issue in this territory. Venice has always been a place that had to be "conquered" by integrating and shaping the environment, first and foremost by combining human-made and natural action leading to the creation of a balance capable of delivering the beauty we still see today. Venice has been possible—and many stories could be told about this—because the whole process that created Venice was inherently sustainable.
Venice always protected, for example, its sources of timber, namely the Cansiglio forests, to ensure the construction of its ships which were a resource for the city's economy, vitality, and wealth. The growth of the trees was in fact disciplined, as well as their processing, so the workers and the activities related to the whole production cycle were safeguarded.
The creation of the Venetian *mariegole*, which collected the statutes of corporations and arts, led to the drafting of regulations and procedures that had to be followed to achieve an integrated process: none of the activities that were carried out in Venice were to harm other sectors, as they were all part of the same system.
Venice's palazzi and buildings are a prime demonstration of this approach. On average, it took decades to build one edifice in Venice. One generation was not enough to complete the task. We know that those who built the first storey of an edifice very rarely saw the finished work.
However, starting from the construction of the first level, the materials, their weight and elasticity, were chosen considering the structural adjustments the construction was due to undergo: so unlike one would think, the focus was not on the inherent solidity of the structures, but rather on their elasticity and continuous balancing on the soft ground on which these buildings still stand today. For example, we have extremely heavy Istrian

Renata C. stone facades, which one would think disadvantageous in terms of foundation elasticity in the ground and that on the contrary are an integral part of this balance.

Therefore, one key element to keep in mind is connected to replacing the concept of elasticity with that of rigidity; these constructions were built over a long period of time, which contributed to avoiding any kind of waste.

The creation of the Venetian-style terraces is the result of recovering and reusing materials on the construction site, whether it be leftover bricks ground up for the foundations, or stones, first crushed and then pounded, used to create these wonderful floorings, which were then treated with oil to comply to the elasticity of the wooden slabs.

The same goes for many other architectural elements; the Republic of Venice regulated the extraction of Istrian stone from the quarries of Orsera by designating step-, windowsill-, and column-quarries, because Istrian stone, which is a compact limestone that well adapts to the lagoon habitat, depending on its origin and features had different uses in Venetian constructions.

Another example is Istrian stone which when extracted is grey, sometimes dark grey. Venetians, however, understood that this compact stone, characterising many monumental city buildings and resistant to the lagoon environment and to continued exposure to marine aerosol, produced a superficial sulphation. Through this natural and unpreventable process, the surface of Istrian stone turns white, becoming resistant and very pleasing to the eye. It is a long-term process, made of several phases and where nothing can be cast off. We see this in the homes, shops, repurposed structures, and private buildings that become public spaces, and vice versa the workshops, the *squeri* that can be turned into music halls.

Renata C. In this context, in my opinion, restoration is an exemplary discipline. Because only traditional buildings can be restored. This aspect is interesting because a brick wall can undergo a like-for-like repair, extending its life. This type of intervention however cannot be performed on a concrete wall, for instance. The idea that an artifact is inherently endowed with a long lifespan because it holds value, and that it can always be recovered and restored, is something Venetians have always been aware of. The statics of buildings, which I mentioned before, is another even more important aspect: Jacopo Sansovino in 1537 designed a vaulted roof for the Marciana Library, which collapsed, causing him to be sentenced to pay for reconstruction and to rethink the architectural design. Sansovino came from another region and, at first, did not fully understand the urban context of Venice. Andrea Palladio, on the other hand, continued to study the city and found many innovative solutions that were suitable for his buildings.

Davide R. This is very interesting in terms of sustainability, in terms of what we now call "sustainability." Because Sansovino wasn't fully aware of the "grammar of things," and therefore of syntax.

Renata C. Sansovino built on rigidity while instead he should have built relying on elasticity. But the same can be said for Palazzo Ducale. Palazzo Ducale is the opposite of what we think it should be. It's "empty" at the base, with large arches, and full at the top. But besides the visible part of the building we should also consider its foundations, structured with arches that are specular to those on ground level, evenly distributing the load on the soft ground upon which St. Mark's Square and basically of all Venice rests. A truly unique solution.
I'd like to return to the "long-term logic" theme, seeing how everything we do inherently takes on a temporal dimension. So, not only a spatial dimension, but also a temporal one, as well as the deterioration of what has been built. It goes without saying that there can always be a phase of completion when a work has just been finalised, but as soon as the materials are set in place, their deterioration process begins.
This is something that our culture rejects, and which was once fully acknowledged.

Davide R. Yes, it was obvious. Renata talked about mutability, climatic conditions, and a population living on a small piece of land. This small dimension makes it difficult to develop cultivations, although Venice has become home to wonderful vegetable patches and gardens for this very same reason.

A Greater Venice that, throughout its history, has made hospitality—in the sense of displaying itself to the world—her true form of communication, a city extraordinaire in representing herself to those coming from abroad.

After all, Venice is Venice not by chance, it became a Greater Venice also due to the Republic's expansionist action. A Greater Venice that, throughout its history, has made hospitality—in the sense of displaying itself to the world—her true form of communication, a city extraordinaire in representing herself to those coming from abroad. Without even mentioning its great reception potential. Hospitality is a key aspect of Venice, and not just in terms of relationship because, unlike a "tourist," a "guest" is both the host and the hosted, and this entails a relationship between people; tourism, as we understand it today, is passive and does not imply a relationship. This is why we strongly believe that Venice needs hospitality, needs people with a connection to things, not tourism.
Cesare has always been an advocate, a supporter of this aspect, which he has thoroughly analysed, so I will quote him once again: Venice, unfortunately—and this is unsustainable—has become a city of pizzerias with no ovens, and of restaurants with no kitchens.
We need to put this in writing because it is key, because it represents the city as we left it before Covid, before the restoration; today the Covid emergency is ending, and the restoration has been completed. By the way, the metaphor between the end of something and restoration seems very fitting...

Casare B. I agree, I think that we should start from these values, from the Venice we once knew. We do not want Venice to go back to how it was before. It would be a mistake to aim or plan to make it return that way. Everyone made egregious mistakes. So we should take this opportunity to rethink the city precisely along the lines that Renata mentioned, that is, starting from its unique and distinctive environment.
Tourism is currently geared towards experiential tourism: hopefully we won't go back to large numbers of tourists for at least the next two or three years. But if we continue to invest in that direction we will just

Casare B. be wasting our energies because there won't be any future; it may not happen in two or four years, perhaps in five or six, but in any case that pace is not sustainable; therefore it would be a losing battle right from the outset. We need to start from the values that created this city which are, from my point of view and that of other colleagues who have invested in quality catering, quality tourism, hospitality, and the city's unique environment and landscape.

We need to start from the values that created this city which are [. . .] quality tourism, hospitality, and the city's unique environment and landscape.

The lagoon...
In ancient times everything was connected, linked, governed.
The city, the idea of the city, its architecture once were governed, while now, the city we see nowadays is completely unmanaged, the lagoon has been totally abandoned and in the last thirty or forty years, there has been no management.
Venice has been used and exploited. We need to restart from the lagoon environment and landscape with a humble, calm, and clear approach.
The tourist flows we have known won't return for the next two or three years, we will not see those large masses again. Yet we will have proximity tourism, people that, spare me the term, are more educated, who know how to relate.

Davide R. Indeed, the concept of education is a fundamental, universal concept, and bad education is something to be rejected, it is unviable.
We must start attributing meaning to this word: bad education is "unsustainable." Masses are not sustainable in Venice, Venice needs men and women who are aware. Because when you use the word masses, you are giving a vague definition of a cluster of people who become depersonalised and no longer aware of themselves becoming something else. That is what a mass is. And the presence of masses of people is inconceivable in Venice. It is inconceivable in general, especially in Italy, because although Venice is the ultimate example of fragility, flexibility, and adjustment capability, all of Italy is fragile . The Cinque Terre, Amalfi... The territory must be governed. So my question is: how important are study and research?

Renata C. Research and study are inherent to this city, first of all because there has been a long period, from the fall of the Republic of Venice up to today, during which we have gradually forgotten what La Serenissima had always stood for. Just think of the development of the arts; Cesare mentioned hospitality, and you spoke about representativeness. It is a well-known fact that mirror production was a highly developed sector in Venice. It was not a matter of vanity, but because anyone who owned so much wealth, Venetian merchants and citizens, felt that through their building facades, their clothing, their relations, they had to affirm a representativeness that equalled what he they had received from the city, paying homage to it.
The mindset we should adopt nowadays should be about giving back as much as possible to the community, not only through the activities, for example, of a large research institution such as Fondazione Giorgio Cini, but above all through what our universities and the fields of research can achieve.
The feeling of ongoing restitution should be pervasive. Therefore, studying and researching are continuous and permanent representations of progress and open-mindedness; it is unthinkable that what we study and learn from the past does not have or does not constitute per se a principle of innovation. If

Renata C. we can study a seven-century history of an emblematic organisation such as the city of Venice, it means this is a treasure chest filled with topics, opportunities for exchange and dialogue, and ultimately a variety of perspectives that spreading from Venice, may become a primary form of dissemination...
The emblematic and iconic value of Venice is generated by the presence of many opportunities; why does the whole world think that this city is extraordinary? Because everyone recognises in it something pertaining to their culture, their origins, their skills, even just their perspective of the world. Therefore studies and research are the means by which we give back, in a never-ending process what we continue to discover. Using new tools? Yes, absolutely. With advanced technologies? Most certainly. We would not have the digital copy of Paolo Veronese's *Wedding at Cana* at Fondazione Giorgio Cini if our experiment, if our investigation had not encompassed the scene of Napoleon coming to Venice, cutting the painting and taking it to the Louvre, displaying it opposite the *Mona Lisa*, leaving an unbridgeable void, until the day we had the suitable technologies to reunite this painting with its Palladian context, for which it was originally created, ultimately achieving an overall greater cultural fruition.
The same can be said for music, whether early, classical, or contemporary music, and for melodrama and acting in general, for the history of art and of Venice and its relationship with the East, which is still nowadays very important, but that today is still in search of a process for a mutual and continuative dialogue. These are the fruits of study and research, and this is what makes us Venetians, and many other people, regardless of origin and residence, citizens of this city.

Davide R. This happens because research and study become a place, a territory of sorts, where everyone can gather, those who carry out the research and those who study.

Renata C. Yes, those who carry out research and study, and also those who disseminate the results of these activities.

Davide R. This is the city where the largest publishing industry in the world developed when print was first invented. And for this reason, the Al Covo restaurant is truly an agency for cultural promotion of the territory. Why? Because behind its fundamental objective, which is to offer refreshments, food and beverages, to its guests paired with all the rites that come with a host-patron relationship, there is an idea, that is first and foremost to employ the skills of small-scale workers like fishermen, cheesemakers, and bakers. In other words, those who express themselves through the quality of their expertise, here find a place of expression. This is one possible approach to the concept of sustainable hospitality. I would like Cesare to expand on this topic because there are at last other projects and, as Renata says, it is something that continues and makes progress. To evolve, *tradere* in Latin means "to take beyond," so tradition means to continuously evolve. If accumulated knowledge does not change on a daily basis, there will never be a tradition, but it will only be something that, over time, will become effete and extinct.

Casare B. Yes, that's true Davide. The city has been virtually decimated, it has lost its residents, and this is a major problem. And what has this led to? To the loss of the city's memory, its traditions, with the result that we found ourselves in a city that was only a mere representation of itself...
Maybe it was like that also in the seventeenth or in the eighteenth century. Venice has probably always been the representation of something, but at the time it represented great ideas, a great vision; now these great ideas are no longer there, what remains is this abstract representation,

Casare B. without the memory of its inhabitants, without its soul, without its people. Why does any of this have something to do with catering? Because if the city loses its memory there is the risk of also losing its heritage, which alone is not enough to produce quality. But at least it is a starting point for offering high-quality hospitality.

The role that in my opinion, the catering must have, is twofold: that of keeper of traditions and of narrator. Keeper of traditions, because as you said, the city has a catering industry with no cooks and no kitchens, because the last administrations, and the previous ones, mismanaged the entire hospitality industry. Deregulation allowed the opening of places that outsource cooking and sell precooked food, passing it off as "original Italian food," "original pizza," or "real Italian pizza." They don't even have the equipment to cook these food, not even an oven to make proper pizza, nor the right people, since they don't employ real cooks or pizza makers.

The role that in my opinion, the catering must have, is twofold: that of keeper of traditions and of narrator.

So, the first role the catering must take on is that of keeper, to keep traditions alive because they are slowly fading. We no longer remember what they were about, where the recipes came from, their ingredients. The other role it must take on is that of capable narrator. There should always be some form of storytelling about the food that is offered. This is an emblematic city that attracts the whole world: Americans or Australians do not relate to products as we do. The word *polenta* means nothing to them, bittersweet fragrances, the smell of vinegar, for example: it's up to us to create a narrative about these things. That is when an interesting situation emerges: food becomes a small "experience." This is the latest trend in tourism, this is what they are asking for, a gastronomic experience, experiential travel… This is why, and I repeat myself here, I found that what you said about the environment, about the understanding of the environment and landscape was spot on.

Davide R. I totally agree, because to experience means to learn. During the Renaissance there were two ways of learning: *non avi canoscenza sanza esperienza* (there can't be knowledge without experience) and literature. Leonardo da Vinci called himself an *omo sanza lettere* (an illiterate man), and lived only on experience, in the sense that he was always focused on what he was pursuing and did not waste a single moment; his keen observation however always translated into knowledge and science in the highest sense of the word, whereby experience led to knowledge, and in turn knowledge led to new experiences, to new creativity.

Venice has always been a very fluid, international city, hence Fondaco dei Tedeschi, Fondaco dei Turchi, and people from Armenia, Greece, Genoa, Modena.

This takes us back to the meaning of the word experience in the sense of knowledge; to offer people an experience, thus knowledge, we must be able to channel it, we must become masters, teachers, if we want to leave a mark. The fact that Venice has been abandoned by the Venetians is a major problem… Venice has always been a very fluid, international city, hence Fondaco dei Tedeschi, Fondaco dei Turchi, and people from Armenia, Greece, Genoa, Modena. Venice was welcoming. We must not forget this.

Casare B. Diversity was perceived as a resource.

Davide R. Precisely. The city cannot live on hospitality alone, it must return to relying on other forms of business, which here can find craftsmanship, but also open up to the digital world; Venice must also rediscover its original, active, planning drive, that is with people designing and creating, like greengrocers, fishermen, jobs that are life projects. All this then turns into a fabric. Now I would like Cesare to conclude our conversation by telling us about his extraordinary earthbound project.

Casare B. Yes. Earlier I was telling you about how we need to restart from our environment and territory, and for over one year and a half we have been working on an innovative project. We created an association, an agricultural company whose members are restaurant owners, and we have rented two hectares of land at Sant'Erasmo where we have started growing organic vegetables, but our goal is to eventually switch to a biodynamic practice. Our project is one of a kind in our area, and we use it to supply our own restaurants and those of others with our products. Our goal is to reconnect our work to the environment and its soil. This has already been done in other regions, such as Piedmont and Liguria, two areas that have plenty of land suitable for organic and biodynamic cultivations. This has never been done in Venice. We are the first.

Davide R. Could scholarly contexts, the world of research, make space for this kind of activity? We talked about art earlier, but what can we say about this intimately connected activity...

Renata C. We know that, probably, Venice's fortune was originally connected to medicinal herbs. But the biodiversity of the lagoon and its islands, in terms of food and other aspects, is a key factor in maintaining the natural balance, developing new projects. Nettles and many other wild herbs were extensively used in many dishes; nowadays, except in rare cases, it is hard to imagine those wonderful combinations, because we have lost knowledge of them. This also applies to wines for example.
The Republic of Venice knew very well which were the—few—wines it could produce and, just as well, knew the commercial routes of other types of wine that were appreciated by its population. Malvasia is a typical example. In the past, in Venice there were roughly 120–130 places where you could drink different types of malvasia wines. Only a few people were authorised to sell Malvasia and only at certain times of the day; the storage of malvasia wines in barrels followed specific regulations. Malvasia came from Greece. Venice imported huge quantities of it up to the point that the Republic reached the monopoly of this trade. Even today cultivations are an important asset for the insular environment, for the soil of this lagoon extending for six hundred square kilometres, the largest in Europe, home to the largest lagoon habitat... The same can be said for fishing and fish farms, the flora, and the fauna.

Davide R. Speaking about fish, Renata reminded me of Andrea Calmo's letters. He was a man who really enjoyed food, shrimps in particular... "*gh'avemo magna' tanti che i scòrsi dei gamberi arrivava a i ginocchi*" (we ate so many shrimps that we were up to our knees in shells). Calmo made an impressively long list of lagoon fish and birds. What's left of that variety of flora and fauna today is very little...

Renata C. Some things need to be rediscovered, looked at with different eyes.

Davide R. I agree. This is interesting... I mean the concepts that you have brought up: the importance of memory, of maintenance, of storytelling, and the importance of study and research.

Renata C. If we look at Veronese's *Wedding at Cana*, with its 165 figures gathered at a large banquet, now we are able to identify—also thanks to the studies that were carried out on the painting—the dishes being served to the guests. The painting captures a moment in life. A great feast, a banquet, attended by the poor and the rich, donning simple and lavish clothes. The musical instruments and the various furnishings were an integral part, and culture and hospitality were not separated, they shared a similar meaning and were connected in many ways. In my opinion this aspect is key and we also find it in the Greater Venice, or even in the villas on the Republic's *terraferma*, a combination where craftsmanship led to the best results, ranging from fabrics, musical instruments, glass objects, furnishings, etc.

Davide R. The smells.

Renata C. Yes, of course, the smells too... everything combines in the sharing of food because it is a real, radical experience: it should never be something "quick." But nowadays we always perceive it as something fast or fleeting. But at that time food was a fundamental part of people's lives.

Davide R. Today unfortunately, without being aware of it we are used to separating culture and hospitality, but actually it is only one, great culture. This is the strength that Venice, as well as other extraordinary Italian realities, has always had: a unitary vision, the governing of things. Therefore our

Davide R. conversation could truly stand as a small metaphor of the will to reunite these two aspects leading to a governing of the things of the city. It is a new way of facing the problem, and offers a new and necessary vision so that this city may return to being a Greater Venice. A Greater Venice of values, not of numbers.

Casare B. A city that is not only about representation. But also about...

Davide R. Experience, communication, storytelling, memory, research, and study, all of this, and above all, of good will.

Renata C. We are sitting on a huge and extraordinary treasure. We're talking about Venice in these terms because it is really difficult to find anything that is not part of the Venice experience, therefore we all feel dwarfed... We are "dwarfs," compared to the greatness of Venice, that we fragment because it makes it easier for us to settle in this kind of framework. But things are not that way. This is where in my opinion there is plenty of work to do... Traditionally, Venice has had centuries-old families living in it; the inhabitants of this city had been here for generations. So our duty is to rediscover the wealth and quality of all the elements Venice is composed of in order to repopulate and revitalise it.

Davide R. For this reason, it is imperative to create and restore those activities that make a city alive. If we do not bring back the know-how we won't bring back life. This aspect is crucial.

HUMANITY. BEYOND THE CONSTRUCTION SITE

DIANA BAGNOLI

VIETATO
L'INGRESSO
AI NON ADDETTI

SALA
RIUNIONI
D.L.

GRUPPO

Kapriol

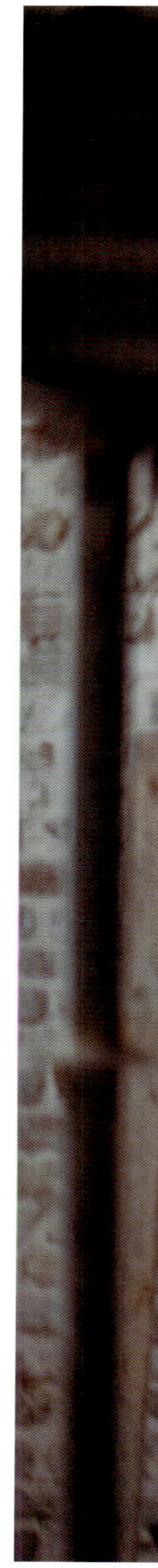

SACAIM

CARNELOS
CARNELOS PIER PAOLO
Falegname & Restauratore
Royal Red

ANTI-FOG
COATED

san marco

LUIGINO FABRIS
GENERALI

GENERALI

Dussmann Service
VALERIO

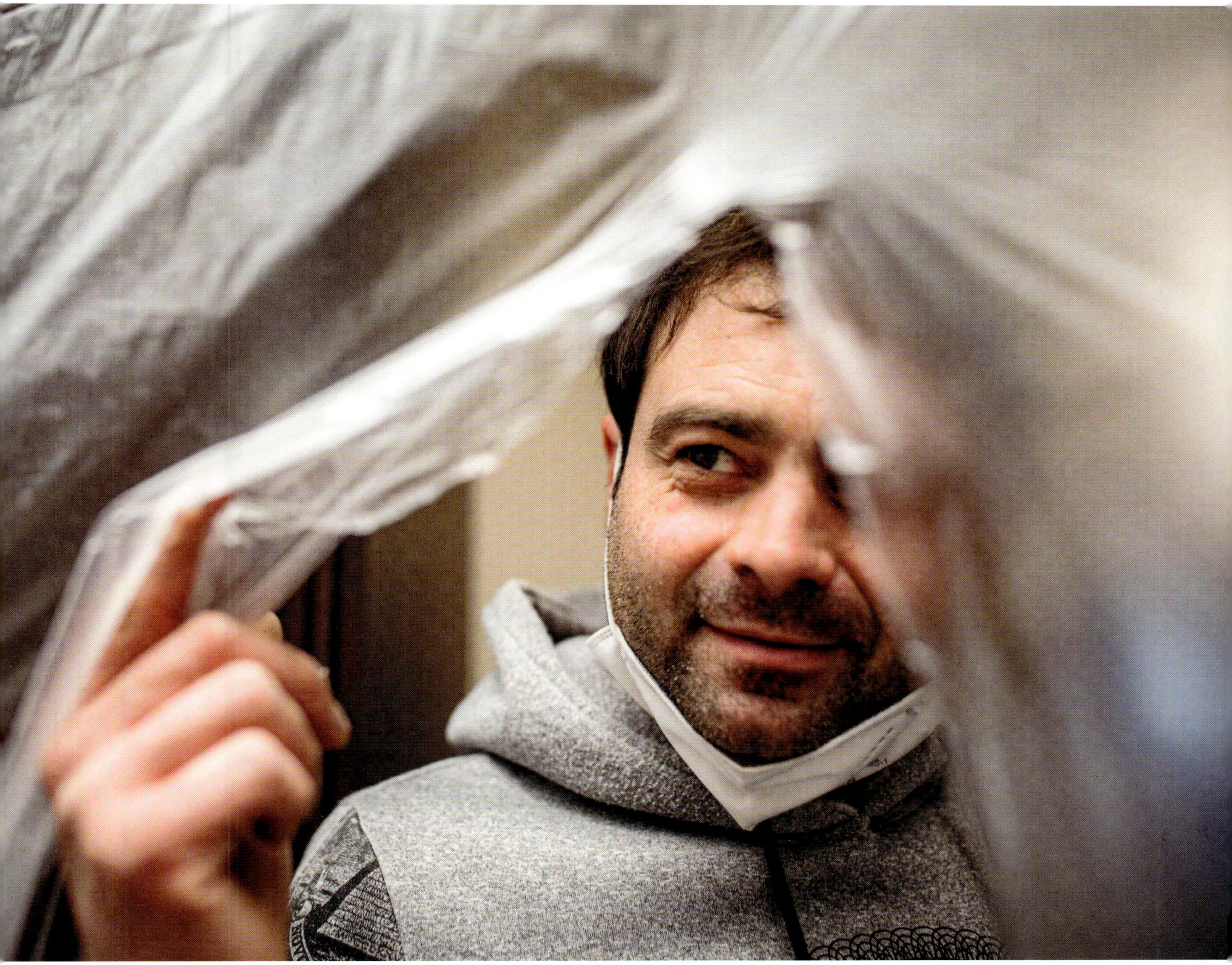

Sei una persona **curiosa**?

InLove

BEAUTY AND HUMAN FLOURISHING

ARTHUR BROOKS

I have travelled constantly for the past thirty-eight years, starting when I left university at age nineteen to work as a touring classical musician, until today as I lecture on the subject of the science of happiness. Over the course of these travels, I have been privileged to visit many of the world's most famous destinations—the places marketed as "The World's Oldest" *this* and "The World's Largest" *that*.

I'll be honest: these destinations generally over-promise and underdeliver. There's a little bit of Disneyland (which calls itself "the happiest place on earth") in the marketing. But sometimes—very occasionally—they *exceed* the PR hype. The Alaskan glaciers are an example of this; so are the pyramids of Giza.

And then, there's Venice, which is in a class by itself. I first visited the famous city at the age of twenty-one during a concert tour. From the very first moment, it took my breath away. A perfect Renaissance city in the water, chock-a-block with magnificent churches and palaces, yet bustling with modern commerce. Its beauty and strangeness allure me back time and again.

The crown jewel of Venice is St. Mark's Square, where all the senses come together, mixing the greatest achievements of Renaissance architecture with some of the finest music in the Western tradition, all in the context of the propagation of spiritual truths. The eleventh-century Italo-Byzantine basilica was a source of inspiration for both composers and painters. It is flanked by opulent palaces, perfectly preserved, the most notable being the exquisite Procuratie Vecchie, built in the early sixteenth century to house the dignitaries of the Republic of Venice.

Venice is a model of human flourishing, where beauty meets human ingenuity, experienced not as a museum exhibit, but rather as beauty should be experienced: in the course of living.

Beauty has many positive effects on human beings. The most obvious is that it provokes deep emotions. These start with what we all want: happiness. Scholars demonstrated this in a 2015 study of 258 British senior citizens by separating them randomly into two groups—one assigned to group singing, and the others to ordinary leisure activities.[1]

They found that after three months, the singers scored 47 percent lower on symptoms of depression, and 13.7 percent higher on mental quality of life.

But happiness increases even when we consume beauty more passively. As three scholars wrote in 2012 in the journal *Urban Design and Planning*, according to surveys, what makes happiness most within reach day in and day out to average citizens is living in an aesthetically beautiful place.[2] This is the central idea behind the philosopher Alain de Botton's famous book *The Architecture of Happiness*,[3] which argues that architecture has a unique role in our well-being.

But de Botton goes further: "There are few harsher indictments against architecture than the sadness

we feel at the arrival of bulldozers," he writes, "for our grief is in almost all cases fuelled more by a distaste for what is to be built than by any hatred of the idea of development itself." Indeed, aesthetics stimulate more than mere good feelings. Even beauty provokes in us the full range of experience and emotion.[4] A sad song inspires sadness, which you sometimes seek out as a strangely ecstatic experience.[5] One study from 2012 even found that the experience of fear makes art seem all the more sublime.[6]

It is easy in our world of modern efficiency to relegate these aesthetic benefits as diversions from reality. Indeed, I have heard Venice described as a kind of "Renaissance Disneyland": a place where one finds relief from the "real world." The belief that realism is devoid of beauty—especially in architecture—reached its apogee in the Soviet Union, where entire cities were built in depressing, grey concrete blocks.

But in fact, this idea about reality is upside down, according to the nineteenth-century philosopher Arthur Schopenhauer. What we might today call the hamster wheel of ordinary life routines, he more grandiosely dubbed the "Wheel of Ixion," named after the king in Greek mythology who tried to seduce Zeus' wife Hera and was punished by being bound to a great fiery wheel, spinning for eternity.[7] This wheel was, for Schopenhauer, a metaphor for the worldly rat race, which was governed by an attribute he called "will" (*Wille*)—our mindless drive for worldly success. Will subjugates us, turning us into *homo economicus*, and condemns our days and years to drudgery.

In some respects, will is a capitulation to reality, a response to the fact that each of us must meet our basic needs. But Schopenhauer argued that will in fact leads to a form of delusion, in which our focus becomes so narrow that we no longer perceive objective reality.[8] We obsess over our everyday experiences, which are small and subjective, swinging us thoughtlessly between desire and boredom.[9] Art, by contrast, forces us to stop looking through the soda straw of our workaday lives and see the world as it truly is.[10] In experiencing art, we contemplate and absorb universal ideas, instead of fixating on the stultifying minutiae of me, me, me.

Engaging with art after worrying over the minutiae of your routine is like looking at the horizon after you've spent too long staring intently at a particular object: your perception of the outside world expands. This refocusing enables what the Stanford neuroscientist Andrew Huberman calls panoramic vision, widening our perspective of true reality by allowing us to see more.[11] In addition to increasing awareness of the broader world, Huberman shows that narrow vision heightens our fear response, but widening our perspective lowers stress.[12]

Art opens our mental aperture and provides relief from the narrow tedium of will. "The true work of art leads us [. . .] [to] that which exists perpetually and time and time again in innumerable manifestations," Schopenhauer wrote in 1851.[13]

Think of a time when you heard a piece of music and wanted to cry. Or recall the flutter of your heart as you stared at a delicate, uncannily lifelike sculpture. Or more to the point, the dizziness as you emerge from a narrow side street onto St. Mark's Square in Venice. Odds are, you didn't feel as if the object of beauty was a narcotic, deadening you. Instead, it was probably a visceral awakening, much like the shock from a lungful of pure oxygen after breathing smoggy air.

"Put usefulness first, and you lose it," said the philosopher Sir Roger Scruton.[14] "Put beauty first, and what you do will be useful forever." We need more art in our lives to experience life fully, to be useful in the most transcendent sense, and to see things as they truly are. Better yet, we need to be fully immersed in beauty as often as we can. This can be metaphorical, as when music envelops us, or literal when we walk inside the Procuratie Vecchie.

What activity could make the most of this physical immersion into beauty? Perhaps an exploration of oneself—of one's strengths as a human being. And this is precisely the focus of the interactive experience promoted by The Human Safety Net within its historic building. The experience could be defined as a study of one's own potential, while standing within an example of humankind's potential to create timeless beauty. It is difficult to imagine a better opportunity to be fully alive.

[1] S. Coulton, S. Clift, A. Skingley, J. Rodriguez. 2015. "Effectiveness and cost-effectiveness of community singing on mental health-related quality of life of older people: Randomised controlled trial." *British Journal of Psychiatry*, 207(3): 250–255.

[2] A. Goldberg, K. M. Leyden, T. J. Scotto. 2012. "Untangling what makes cities liveable: happiness in five cities." *Proceedings of the Institution of Civil Engineers. Urban Design and Planning*, 165(3): 127–136.

[3] A. De Botton. 2006. *The Architecture of Happiness*. New York.

[4] P. G. Hunter, E. G. Schellenberg, U. Schimmack. 2010. "Feelings and Perceptions of Happiness and Sadness Induced by Music." *Psychology of Aesthetics, Creativity, and the Arts*, 4(1): 47–56.

[5] L. O. Lundqvist, F. Carlsson, P. Hilmersson, P. N. Juslin. 2009. "Emotional responses to music: experience, expression, and physiology." *Psychology of Music*, 37(1): 61–90; S. Khalfa, D. Schon, J. L. Anton, C. Liégeois-Chauvel. 2005. "Brain regions involved in the recognition of happiness and sadness in music." *Neuroreport*, 16(18): 1981–1984.

[6] J. E. Eskine, N. A. Kacinik, J. J. Prinz. 2012. "Stirring Images: Fear, Not Happiness or Arousal, Makes Art More Sublime." *Emotion (Washington, D.C.)*, 12(5): 1071–1074.

[7] A. Schopenhauer. 1883. *The World as Will and Idea*. Translated by Haldane and Kemp. London, 260.

[8] Ibidem, 240.

[9] P. Euron. 2019. "Chapter 16 Schopenhauer." In *Aesthetics, Theory and Interpretation of the Literary Work*. Leiden.

[10] S. Roehr, C. Janaway. 2014. "Chapter XIX On the Metaphysics of the Beautiful and Aesthetics." In *Schopenhauer, Parerga and Paralipomena: Short Philosophical Essays*. Cambridge.

[11] J. Wapner. 16 November 2020. "Vision and breathing may be the secrets to surviving 2020." *Scientific American*. Retrieved from https://www.scientificamerican.com/article/vision-and-breathing-may-be-the-secrets-to-surviving-2020/.

[12] L. D. Salay, N. Ishiko, A. D. Huberman. 2018. "A midline thalamic circuit determines reactions to visual threat." *Nature (London)*, 557(7704): 183–189.

[13] A. Schopenhauer. *Essays and Aphorisms*. Edited and with an introduction by R. J. Hollingdale, London, 1970.

[14] R. Scruton. 2018. "Why Beauty Matters." *The Monist*, 101(1): 9–16.

GENERALI AND VENICE: A PARTNERSHIP FOR PEOPLE, PLACES, AND THE PLANET

SIMON ANHOLT

As a lifelong Italophile, married to an Italian, with a degree in Italian literature, I suppose that Venice has always meant much more to me than just a desirable foreign tourist destination. To me it is one of the cardinal points of my European identity—something that Brexit can never take away from me—and one of the high points of human civilisation.

So when in 2014 I was invited by Generali to develop a corporate social purpose strategy for the group, I admit that Generali's long connection with La Serenissima was an important part of what immediately interested me.

But I couldn't help asking: "why me?"

I hadn't worked in the private sector for more than twenty years, having specialised in working with the governments of nations, cities and regions. What's more, this sounded like a Corporate Social Responsibility (CSR) project, an area in which I had very little experience.

Generali however made it clear to me that the standard recipe of corporate virtue-signalling and greenwashing was not what they were looking for. They didn't want to *look* good, they wanted to *make themselves useful*. And why me? Because this project was as much about a place as it was about a company: the place being, of course, Venice.

My approach to enhancing the reputations of places had long been based on the principle that countries, regions and cities are judged by what they do—and above all, what they do for humanity and the planet, the world *outside* their own borders—rather than what they say about themselves. Venice, for example, didn't become one of the most admired cities on the planet because it was good at self-promotion: it is admired because it is admirable. As simple as that.

So the challenge was this: how could Generali help Venice become more and more admirable to more and more people around the world?

Nobody could resist a challenge like that, and I agreed to help.

Devising an environmental, social and governance (ESG) strategy—as we would call it today—for a large international corporation is no simple matter, partly because there really is no broadly accepted understanding of what ESG really means in practice, or how to measure its success; and partly because it isn't always easy to find pro-social activities that clearly contribute to the corporation's mandate of providing value to shareholders. In consequence, each corporation must make its own rules of engagement as it moves forward.

Of course, some easily recognisable ESG habits and patterns of behaviour have evolved during the last ten to fifteen years, but not many of them can be proved to have achieved much tangible value either for the corporations themselves or for the social causes they attempt to address, so they are probably a better guide for what to avoid than what to emulate.

What still perturbs me is the *tonality* of some current ESG activity: communications in the field are still distinguished by a self-conscious tone of voice which balances precariously between bragging and fake humility. At its worst, this pious, moralising tone implies a confusion of motivations and a deep moral uncertainty.

In a period when the very existence of a social purpose strategy, as an activity that is still quite distinct from ordinary corporate behaviour, is still somewhat remarkable, it's not surprising its practitioners tend to feel the need to draw attention to it, and to "add to its value" by promoting it. But as ESG embeds itself more and more deeply into corporate strategy and corporate behaviour, as it gradually becomes the "new normal," it is bound to become viewed ever less as a separate activity, and consequently not talked about as if it were the mark of some extraordinary corporate virtue.

It's therefore easy to imagine how much of the tonality of today's ESG activity will soon look very old-fashioned, as we learn to see it neither as a charitable donation to society, nor as a kind of tax imposed by society on corporations, but rather as a straightforward development of good corporate governance. When planning and executing business, we now need to look a little further into the future, embracing such risks and opportunities as climate change, demographic change, social mobility, resource scarcity and species loss. We also need to look a little wider than our conventional supplier and customer base, thus considering the current and future needs of our secondary stakeholders in the developing world and in other regions where we are not yet commercially active.

Now, following multiple challenges to the Washington Consensus, the pandemic, the global economic crisis, and the overwhelming scientific consensus on the causes and implications of climate change, companies are once again forced to realise that they have two feet on the ground wherever

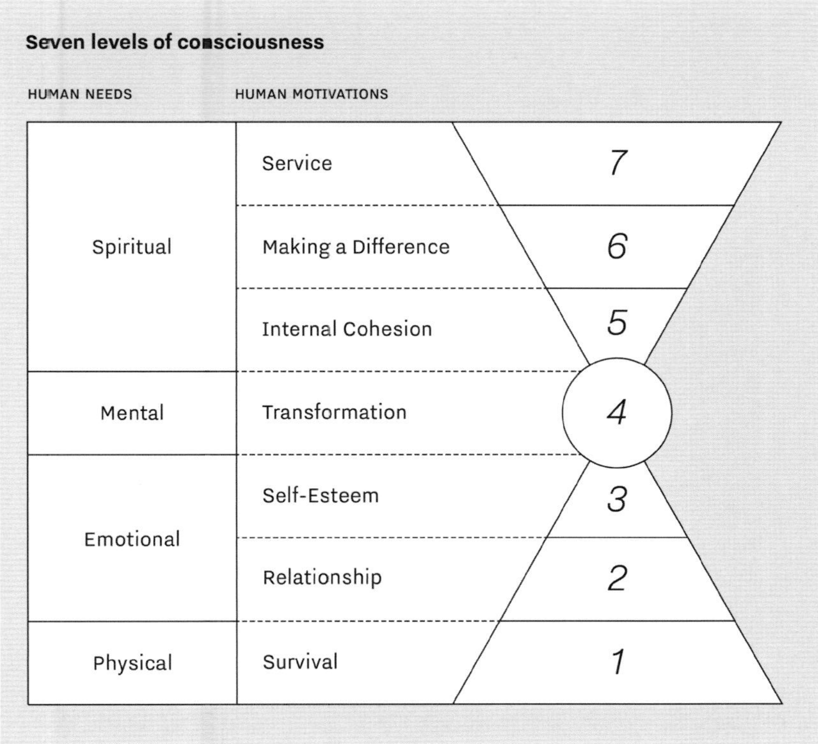

Richard Barrett's *Levels of Consciousness*, www.valuescentre.com.

they operate: a commercial footprint and a social footprint, each carrying certain responsibilities and offering certain opportunities. The mere fact that it employs as many people as the population of a substantial town means that Generali is an actor in society as well as an actor in commerce, and this isn't about guilt or responsibility—it's a simple statement of reality.

Reconciling these two connections with the world, and ensuring that they are in harmony and mutually beneficial, is one of the most important tasks facing corporations today.

Every corporation is therefore a heart with two chambers: the social and the commercial. They must beat as one, and there are risks if one is more highly developed than the other: if the corporate side is more effective and sophisticated and prominent than the social, it runs the risk of losing trust amongst employees and customers; if the social side is more effective and sophisticated and prominent than the commercial, it runs the risk of commercial failure.

One useful model for understanding the journey which companies such as Generali have been making is Barrett's *levels of consciousness* model), itself adapted from Abraham Maslow's well-known Hierarchy of Needs: its application to corporations and the ESG agenda has been pointed out by Volans in the UK.

Using this model, it is clear that the corporations currently most active in the ESG field tend to be at Level 6, a level at which their ESG activities are more professional and more genuinely useful to society than before, but the corporation still tends to frame and promote this activity as an additional, explicitly moral, voluntary and transactional activity—"giving something back to society," rather than a normal component of its everyday business, where the fundamental purpose of the organisation is to serve society (Level 7).

In 2014, Generali was undoubtedly at the beginning of this new journey, and depending on which part of its operations one considered, was somewhere between Levels 3 and 5; as a whole, it probably averaged out at around Level 4.

The aim of pursuing an ESG agenda, we agreed, was to give people around the world simple reasons to feel glad that Generali exists; to welcome its presence as a social actor, and thus to accord it a certain preference as a corporate actor.

So The Human Safety Net, and several alternative projects which I developed together with Simone Bemporad and Emma Ursich over the course of several months, were framed as a series of responses to the most basic question: how can we best match the strengths, abilities and resources of the corporation with the needs of society?

As companies become more adept at creating these synergies, ESG will soon merge into, and become indistinguishable from, practical corporate stewardship, and as this happens, the way that it's planned, executed and communicated will change significantly. My feeling in 2014 was that it would be wise for Generali to pre-empt this now, rather than spend time building structures and capabilities which will look redundant just as they reach maturity.

This is a moment in history where we are re-evaluating the role of the corporation in society, something which appears to happen every few centuries. In fact, as I observed in my 2003 book *Brand New Justice*, these principles have been at the heart of the Italian corporation since early in the fourteenth century, when certain family names emerged as symbols

Venice belongs to all of us, and whatever Generali does for, in and with Venice, will be accepted as a gift to all humanity.

of wealth, trust and integrity: the Buonsignori of Siena—the first major international bank—then the Frescobaldi of Florence, the Ricciardi of Lucca, and later still, the Bardi, Peruzzi and Acciaiuoli families, some of whose business empires employed hundreds of staff in subsidiary offices across Europe and the Middle East and North Africa—the area which today we call EMEA.

In their correspondence and journals, the medieval Italian merchants stress over and over again the importance of creating a good and famous name: to be recognised far and wide as honourable citizens, to play a distinguished part in social and civic life, to support culture and donate to good causes. It's interesting how this aspect of corporate reputation, never forgotten or overlooked by most clever and successful companies, has recaptured the attention of big business in the late twentieth and early twenty-first centuries, and the idea has been relaunched and rebranded as "CSR" or "ESG," as if it were something that had just been invented.

Only an impeccable reputation for probity, substantial resources and success could confer the kind of trust among new clients which ensured the continuation of their business. In every respect, the power of these family banks was identical to modern brands: they acted as a shortcut to an informed buying or investing decision, and stood as a universally-acknowledged proxy for dependability.

Wise people and well-run companies have always understood that their good name is worth more than riches, for the simple reason that it is the necessary basis for continued prosperity. People will only buy from people they know and trust, but as soon as your customer or prospect is more than a day's ride away on horseback—then your good name must somehow be broadcast, and become a byword for trustworthiness. Hence the value of reputation: it is the broadcast of trust. Reputation (which is just another word for brand equity) is the means by which consumers will feel safe about doing business with you even if they have never met you before.

To broadcast trust, said the medieval Italian bankers, one must demonstrate honour and generosity of spirit. Financial services companies like Generali, more than companies in most sectors, need to be trusted, so it is of the greatest importance that they can find ways to *prove* (not to claim—this is about behaviour, not about messages) that their intentions towards society are strikingly honourable and unfailingly generous.

And since Generali's business is global, these generous and honourable intentions must be extended to the whole of humanity.

This position isn't borne out of some dreamy, abstract desire to do good: it's based on an entirely rational observation about human psychology. If you want to do better business, you need to be trusted, and if you want to be trusted, you must demonstrate your trustworthiness.

It is equally important that Generali's honour and generosity must be felt in *society*, not just in the marketplace. This is perhaps particularly important for an insurance business, which needs to forge a relationship with people's whole lives, not just their leisure time, their possessions or their amusement.

The Role of Venice

These are all good reasons to why the decision to partner with a city, especially a city with the global stature of Venice, makes so much sense: it positions Generali and its mission at the heart of people's daily lives, in the places where they live and work, not just the places where they shop.

And because Venice is one of a handful of cities that are globally important through their intrinsic qualities, not because they are very large or very rich or politically powerful, it is more than just a city in Italy—it is undoubtedly part of humanity's shared heritage. Venice belongs to all of us, and whatever Generali does for, in and with Venice, will be accepted as a gift to all humanity.

It is also necessary (and arguably long overdue) to recharge the "brand" of Venice. The city has been feeding off its own reputation for centuries and, apart from the Biennale and certain other notable cultural activities, the last time it added any new elements to its global contribution was quite a long time ago. Simply promoting Venice as a tourist attraction may keep the economic engines running, but no matter how sustainable the tourism *product* itself becomes, the reputational side of the operation is simply not sustainable—you can't keep cutting down the forest, you need to plant new trees.

Just being beautiful and historically important isn't enough: a city must also seek to remain *relevant* in some way to many people in many other parts of the world. These considerations become ever more important as tourism becomes an ever less popular industry for the people who actually live and work in popular tourist destinations. In Venice, Florence, Rome, Amsterdam, Barcelona and numerous other "must-see" cities, we are starting to see a powerful backlash against overtourism and the social, economic and environmental strains it puts on ancient and fragile places. Cities need to find new ways of forging sustainable and mutually beneficial relationships with the outside world that are deeper, more lasting and more equal than simply offering themselves as picturesque backgrounds for trillions of selfies.

In 2005, I launched two annual international polls, measuring people's perceptions of fifty countries (the Anholt Nation Brands Index) and fifty cities (the Anholt City Brands Index). By 2012, the combined database of these surveys had exceeded a billion datapoints, and I decided it would be a good moment to analyse the accumulated data to find out what actually drives the positive reputations of certain highly-regarded countries and cities. Nobody doubts that a good "brand image" is a useful if not essential asset for places. The countries and cities with good images find that everything—from attracting talent, tourists and investors to exporting goods, services and people—is easier and cheaper, while everything is more difficult and more expensive for places with weak or negative reputations. But the root causes of these images had long been something of a mystery: my research conclusively proved that it had nothing to do with self-promotion, and there was no correlation between the strength of any country's image and the amount of money its government spent on public relations, advertising and branding.

My analysis showed that while perceptions of economic success, natural beauty, rich culture and advanced technology can all play a role in the formation—over decades and generations—of a positive place image, these weren't the main drivers. By a wide margin the most significant factor was the perception that the country or city contributed to the world outside its own borders: to humanity and the planet. In other words, domestic success doesn't necessarily correlate with a good image, but positive international impact does. It seems that we all prefer *good* countries and *good* cities: but when I say "good" I mean "good the opposite of selfish," not "good the opposite of bad."

But the "brand personality" of Venice today is no longer about its contribution to the world: to a great extent, it has become defined by its environmental problems. For many people around the world, their associations with Venice are increasingly tinged with anxiety, and an image of fragility and weakness is particularly unsustainable in the longer term. People can't feel constantly sorry for, or guilty about, Venice: at some point they need to start feeling grateful that it exists because it's contributing powerfully to the world in which we all live.

This is why initiatives like The Human Safety Net, closely associated with Venice, and proposed by a company with deep roots in Venice, are so valuable in associating the city with the factors that will continue to fuel its positive image—to grow its brand equity rather than simply spend it.

Let us hope that The Human Safety Net will inspire other organisations to contribute to the standing of the cities in which they operate, and in doing so, increase their own standing.

When it comes to good governance in the age of global challenges, whether we are talking of cities or of companies, it's clear that doing well and doing good are effectively the same thing.

A PLACE TO CALL HOME

EMMA URSICH

A home is made of bricks but human connections are what bring it to life. A home resonates with relationships, memories, care, familiar smells, habits: it can be both a place to tuck away and a springboard from which to engage the world. It is a place that defines us, where we spend so much of our lives and that, since an early age, shapes who we are and how we relate to others.

The Human Safety Net, that over a few years has grown into a global movement of people helping people, is based on the conviction that everybody has a potential and deserves a chance to fulfil it, and on the belief that no matter how big or small, every contribution counts towards transforming lives.

This book is about the people from all over the world who have contributed to making the Procuratie Vecchie a home to The Human Safety Net, that over a few years has grown into a global movement of people helping people, based on the conviction that everybody has a potential and deserves a chance to fulfil it, and on the belief that no matter how big or small, every contribution counts towards transforming lives, by weaving a "human safety net" where all like-minded individuals and organisations are encouraged to join and bring their ideas, time, skills and resources to build something more impactful together.

Such belief informs all the work The Human Safety Net carries out around the world, engaging alongside passionate non-profit organisations and social entrepreneurs to bring about social change, one family, one refugee at a time. The Human Safety Net today is a network of over sixty organisations from twenty-three countries, working on the same challenges: promoting policies and practices to support early childhood development for families living in vulnerable contexts and supporting refugees in creating their path towards employment or entrepreneurship in their country of destination. This effort was initiated by Generali and its people and conceived from the very beginning as an open architecture aiming to unlock the potential of collaborations and partnerships across the profit and non-profit, public and private domains sharing the same values and goals. Our ambition is to activate a chain of people helping people creating a ripple effect like that generated by a drop of water. It seems quite apt for this ripple to reverberate from a city built entirely on water.

Our ambition is to activate a chain of people helping people creating a ripple effect like that generated by a drop of water.

The Human Safety Net has always considered Venice its centre of gravity, even before making the third floor of the Procuratie Vecchie its new home starting in 2022. Members of this network have met and gathered in Venice since the very beginning to exchange and design solutions for its programmes on the ground, year after year expanding the connections within the network, returning home every time inspired and full of energy to test new approaches and reach further together.

With its new home, this approach can now become a permanent working practice, opening up so many new opportunities to reach more people, create new connections, and further opportunities for exchange and debate; to design and amplify attention, understanding, and action around the pressing issues of social inclusion but also more widely around sustainability as the cornerstone for human resilience and wellbeing.

What better place than the fragile, ingenious Venice to discuss how humans can work together to preserve and improve our shared future? It is no coincidence in fact that this city is working to bring its contribution to the global community as "World Capital of Sustainability." There is so much to do and The Human Safety Net is glad to play its part, activating all the potential of its global network from its base in the Procuratie Vecchie, in St. Mark's Square, in an open, permeable city that is by its nature a

What better place than the fragile, ingenious Venice to discuss how humans can work together to preserve and improve our shared future?

symbol to the world.

The third floor of the Procuratie Vecchie is what used to be the servants' quarters of the residences of the Procuratori, with its small rounded windows, called *occhi*, eyes, discreetly looking onto the square and offering precious glimpses of the hubbub below and of the hallmarks of one of the most famous squares in the world. The renovation carried out by David Chipperfield Architects has highlighted the quality of the spaces, bringing out their unique features while making them open, connected and apt for contemporary life and work with striking harmony and balance. This new beginning represents a unique opportunity to bridge the gap between history and future, open and closed spaces, local and global issues by means of the new social mission the renovated spaces will embody. They will come alive every day through the work that will be carried out there, the experiences visitors will engage with, and the events and content people will be able to shape and enjoy.

It is indeed a home full of history and memory spanning more than five hundred years towards which, we as The Human Safety Net, feel a deep connection and responsibility. The magistrates who originally inhabited these spaces, the Procuratori, were in charge, among other things, of administering the private wealth of the city but also of caring and providing for those on the margins of society, orphans, widows and the destitute. Their action was part of a social contract which provided a safety net of sorts. It is meaningful to be able to set up our home in these same spaces, renovating this mission in a way that is fit for the twenty-first century.

For the first time ever, these spaces will be open and freely accessible to the public in a way that has never been possible in this building's long history. All sides of St. Mark's Square now will be available

The magistrates who originally inhabited these spaces, the Procuratori, were in charge, among other things, of administering the private wealth of the city but also of caring and providing for those on the margins of society, orphans, widows and the destitute.

to Venetians and visitors alike, who will have the opportunity to discover the complexity behind the neat facade of the Procuratie Vecchie, creating a new dialogue between open air and closed spaces, spanning from the renewed Royal Gardens and its Human Garden glasshouse, to Palazzo Ducale, the Basilica, the Marciana Library, the Archaeological Museum, the Museo Correr and finally the new home of The Human Safety Net, merging history with the most contemporary of topics.

Visitors to the Procuratie Vecchie's Human Safety Net spaces will have the chance to discover and enjoy them not just as spectators but as active participants in a living and welcoming experience where everybody can become as much a protagonist as they wish and, we very much hope, always feel at home and eager to come back, whenever they feel like it.

Talking about social exclusion is never easy. But real human stories and connections are something the majority of us craves and enjoys. That is why, to talk about our work and amplify our net we have created an exhibition space which starts as an interactive journey into discovering one's own strengths

Chances and situations happen in life, and what is most important is not only what happens but how individuals respond, based on their unique characteristics and life circumstances.

as an individual, and then meeting somebody from The Human Safety Net who is like us, sharing the same personality traits.

What does potential mean? Like sliding doors, chances and situations happen in life, and what is most important is not only what happens but how individuals respond, based on their unique characteristics and life circumstances. The work of The Human Safety Net focuses exactly on this: it aims to unlock individuals' potential, to make a new beginning possible for families and refugees in sustainable and lasting ways. Visitors will be able to discover something about themselves and then, if they so wish, join and become a part of The Human Safety Net.

We have been fortunate to work with two trailblazing social entrepreneurs, Andreas Heinecke and Orna Cohen in shaping the exhibition journey, drawing from their vast experience in engaging people around the topic of social inclusion, starting but not limited to their well-known international franchise called *Dialogue in the Dark*, which turns biases towards disabilities upside down, so it is a

All types of local, national and international events will be held, to foster dialogue around social and sustainable topics, to promote the best of Venice and its value for the world, to make beauty accessible in many artistic forms, from books to music to debates and talks, with the ambition to cater for many different interests under the wing of The Human Safety Net.

blind person who becomes a guide to the visitor. All this has been enhanced by the design of the Migliore & Servetto studio who thoughtfully made the exhibits come to life in a constant dialogue with the spaces, under the artistic direction of Davide Rampello & Partners. I am deeply grateful to them for being a part of this journey and drawing together a new path for the Procuratie Vecchie. I could not have imagined better and more stimulating companions in designing this experience. An Art Studio will complement the main visitor route exploring human potential: artists will alternate to give their vision on human strengths in their own language, different and unexpected each time.

Of course there will be work going on in the Procuratie. People will be trained, connections will be created, programmes will be designed working in synergy with the international and local network around sustainability topics. The Covid pandemic has rewritten the rules of daily work but the value of making great minds meet to create something special together will never be lost, on the contrary probably enhanced and made even more intentional and purposeful.

All types of local, national and international events will be held, to foster dialogue around social and sustainable topics, to promote the best of Venice and its value for the world, to make beauty accessible in many artistic forms, from books to music to debates and talks, with the ambition to cater for many different interests under the wing of The Human Safety Net.

The sudden and prolonged stop to tourism caused by the Covid pandemic has made Venice's dependency on this industry all the more evident. Tourism is of course also one of the city's major issues in terms of strain on resources, conservation and quality of life for its citizens. Bringing a historical space back to life, opening it up for the first time, with a public use as a high-quality place of work and engagement for all people is our contribution to the future of Venice and its sustainability. No one can do this alone but we trust this is a good beginning and we look forward to engaging with like-minded people and organisations to bring this space alive in the most meaningful and resonating way for the city and for all the communities that will be touched by the work happening there, in the true spirit of the Human Safety Net.

AN ENGAGING SPACE. SOCIAL IMPACT THROUGH EXPERIENCE

ICO MIGLIORE and ORNA COHEN
in conversation with
LUCA MOLINARI

Luca M. I will ask you a few very simple and basic questions, to introduce the philosophy and the methodology underpinning the installations on the Procuratie Vecchie top floor in relation to the The Human Safety Net project. Can you start by explaining how you have been working together and what are your main goals in your practice? It's very interesting that two people like you have been contacted to work on this installation, this layout. So, I would like to know more about the work you're doing and about your methodology and vision. So first of all, would you like to introduce yourselves?

A global
movement
Un movimento
globale di
persone che
aiutano persone
DEMO
Think
Lenovo

Orna C. I'm the co-founder of Dialogue Social Enterprise. Our motivation to develop exhibitions is deeply rooted in the mission of our company. We are a social enterprise, which aims to positively change the perception of disadvantaged groups and employ people who have little chance of finding a decent job.
Over the last thirty years we have focused on the blind, deaf and elderly people, who in our exhibitions work as guides, which clearly indicates the purpose we believe this type of projects should have. They are never an end in itself, they do not exhibit anything and they are not meant to be aesthetically pleasing or to convey theoretical knowledge.
The exhibitions *Dialogue in the Dark* (where the mediators are blind people), *Dialogue in Silence* (with deaf and hearing-impaired personnel) and *Dialogue with Time* (with over-seventies mediators) are platforms for encounters between blind and sighted, deaf and hearing, old and young people.
These "dialogue exhibitions" are designed as immersive environments to generate a conversation between people who wouldn't normally meet and interact and that when they seldom do, often find themselves trapped in false preconceptions. They are a platform for encounters to give disadvantaged people, due to age or disability, a chance to present their potential in an impressive way. This creates a personal experience and also a relationship that can change the perception of what we believe is "otherness," "foreign," and "threatening," contributing to prevent exclusion and prejudices.
This approach is not only methodologically different from other exhibitions. Our *Dialogue* exhibitions successfully fulfil our mission only if we transfer our know-how to our worldwide partners and not merely physically move the exhibition from place to place. This activates local communities, ensuring a direct impact in the cities where the exhibitions are held.
In the last ten years alone, we have reached almost eight million people across all the continents and provided an income and recognition to eight thousand disadvantaged people.

Ico M. I am the co-founder, together with Mara Servetto, of the Migliore+Servetto studio, which is headquartered in Milan and operates globally. Since 1997, we have developed over five hundred projects in eighteen different countries, winning numerous prizes and recognitions, including three Compasso d'Oro awards.
We specialise in branding projects and narrative spaces, including museums, exhibitions, and installations, but also urban areas, retail spaces, and structures devoted to hospitality. We approach our projects with a cohesive and, so to speak, holistic vision on all levels, ranging from interior design to graphics, from video to multimedia.
In our process, research and continuous experimentation play a key role, also because of my work as university professor, both at the Design School of the Polytechnic University of Milan, where I teach Interior and Spatial Design, and as Chair Professor at the Dongseo University in Busan, South Korea. At the Polytechnic, starting from the concept of cultural proximity, I founded a research unit in which my students have been involved for several years. Mara Servetto has also been dealing with these topics for some time in Japan, where she teaches at the Joshibi University in Tokyo.
Thus, if I were to try to define the distinctive style of our studio, I would term it as an innovative and experimental approach, based on continuous research: this is the value at the core of our projects, which are uniquely sustainable and inclusive.
In our vision, design provides a connection supporting communication between clients and users of the project, making this communication memorable. Light and technology are our means of choice to make projects poetic and expressive.
Our projects are conceived in relation to their context and users, conveying even complex content in engaging and narrative ways. We have adopted this method for important cultural venues in Italy and other European countries, such as

Ico M. the Egyptian Museum in Turin, the Chopin Museum in Warsaw, the ADI Design Museum in Milan, and also for several installations and exhibitions, such as the Italian pavilion at XXII Triennale di Milano Exhibition in 2019 entitled *Broken Nature*. On that occasion, we created a visionary library display of scientific knowledge expressing the multidisciplinary approach of the Polytechnic University of Milan, to which the Italian pavilion was dedicated.
This is how we approached the design of The Human Safety Net three-thousand-square-meters headquarters at the Procuratie Vecchie, creating a cohesive and integrated vision that generated the project for both the exhibition itinerary and all other spaces, from the cafeteria to the co-working and reception areas. With this in mind, we also designed the furnishings, as well as the display panels for communication and orientation, videos, and multimedia installations.

Orna C. We believe in John Dewey's "learning-by-doing" approach.
Or in other words, we try to offer the public a meaningful and lasting experience to improve self-reflection and self-perception. The main challenge was incorporating our approach to support The Human Safety Net's mission and communicating with the public. Concretely speaking: what should an exhibition setting where visitors play an active role and become an object and a subject of the project, look like? How can we spark people's interest in learning more about The Human Safety Net's vision and mission?
How can we provide a lasting experience that may change people's perception of themselves from passive consumers/spectators at an exhibition to active contributors/communicators in society?
With Ico we have tackled this challenge from different angles. His team was in charge of the outer appearance, assuring an aesthetic and well-designed environment, while we tried to envision an itinerary that would have an emotional and cognitive impact on viewers. This collaboration gave place to an incessant dialogue between form and interaction, aesthetics and engagement.

Ico M. The design process required non-stop discussions, which allowed us to turn the emotional and cognitive concept, conceived by Orna and her team, into an actual exhibition itinerary: we created a narrative, a sequence of installations for visitors who are thus encouraged to take their time while enjoying the displays. We not only designed the exteriors of each space; we also focused on content, trying to convey the message and the identity of The Human Safety Net and to turn the Dialogue Social Enterprise proposal into spaces and installations, into contexts where all dimensions of design would converge, including graphics, multimedia, materials, furnishings, and light.
We viewed the exhibition project as a progression of experiences that increase the self-awareness of visitors and their perception of the world. It's something real, which acts on the senses, memory, and gives rise to positive emotions. The outcome, so to speak, is something in-between a science and technology museum and an anthropological experience, but the most stimulating aspect of it all is that people during this experiential journey are invited to look inward. A challenge that through this project we have transformed into an opportunity. As my teacher and mentor Achille Castiglioni used to say: "We do not design objects or spaces, but behaviours." And that's what we wanted to achieve in this extraordinary place.
Here technology is obviously pervasive, but it does not prevail over content; it is a fundamental medium, but it never replaces storytelling or direct experience, indeed it supports it. Everything is intuitive and quite simple.

The outcome, so to speak, is something between a science and technology museum and an anthropological experience, but the most stimulating aspect of it all is that people during this experiential journey are invited to look inward.

Luca M. And what kind of experience would you like to deliver with this project?

Orna C. It has been a long process. We worked on several concepts for The Human Safety Net, and in the end the approach we chose was to create an experience that would create a shift from "me" to "we." The Human Safety Net is about empowering other people. It's about human potential. All of us have potential. Thus, we choose positive psychology as our theoretical frame.
The American psychologists Martin Seligman and Christopher Peterson have developed a very interesting assessment method. It's called VIA (Values in Action) and provides a list of character strengths. VIA is universal and can be applied to all humans, anywhere in the world, and it is based on the idea that character strengths are inherent to all of us, and that they can be strengthened over time, an approach which perfectly matches The Human Safety Net philosophy.
We thought of giving visitors an opportunity to explore some of the twenty-four strengths listed in the VIA classification. The goal is to identify everyone's top strengths. Later on, the visitor can meet (through a video) a protagonist of The Human Safety Net, who shares his or her same top strength, in a sort of speed dating dynamic. The encounter is virtual, but through the character similarities the two share, it becomes personal. The visitor is inspired to learn more about that person, and the work he or she is doing as part of The Human Safety Net. The entire experience becomes personal: it starts with the

Orna C. identification of one's potential, followed by the encounter with a like-minded person, who shares the same potential. This experience helps one understand how everyone can contribute to better the conditions of marginalised communities. It provides, this is our hope, inspiration to start a journey as a social activist and help people who deserve empathy and support.

Luca M. And how has this vision, this approach, been translated into a physical space?

Ico M. I believe that in The Human Safety Net project we intertwined two specific qualities of the studio: on the one hand, expertise in designing cultural venues and, on the other, the ability to define the role of users who will move inside the new "The Human Safety Net home" aiming to make their experience, in terms of encounter and visit, memorable. We never envision spaces as static: we conceive them as narrative "devices" inviting people to interact and join a dialogue, welcoming them in a protective but also proactive way, stimulating knowledge and curiosity.
Needless to say, we integrated The Human Safety Net's vision into this process. Thus, we worked to build a space which, at multiple levels and with different functions, would convey a coherent and univocal message: the Foundation's mission. And we did this considering that the whole project was to relate to a context such as St. Mark's Square, and an exceptional venue, the Procuratie Vecchie building, completed in 1538 and now fully restored by David Chipperfield Architects.
Our goal was to transform this place into The Human Safety Net's "home," with all the prerogatives this term—so common, but also so symbolic—implies; a place where everyone would feel welcome, yet with a contemporary, open, and intimate quality to it.
A space where people move like figures against a carefully designed and organised background, acting as lead characters in a play.
To this end, whenever it was possible, we decided to use natural light coming from the skylights and the oval *oculi* windows along the walls, without creating a dark artificially lit itinerary. We wanted the space to maintain a dialogue with the world outside, with the city around it, remaining as open as possible.

Luca M. Can you tell me something more about the style you chose for this exhibition? As you explained very well, it's an itinerary where performative aspects meet experience, which starts with the individual activating an exchange with the space. So, how is this exhibition structured, managed, and organised?

Orna C. The exhibition has been structured as a three-act journey framed by a prologue and an epilogue.
The prologue introduces the subject of the exhibition in a simple and straightforward way. It sets the tone and the pace, preparing visitors for the journey they are about to embark on. Visitors understand the concept and learn why The Human Safety Net created the exhibition. The prologue starts with a series of questions: what makes you happy? Are you a curious person? What inspires you most? Have you reached your full potential? Questions are a good way to open up to a subject. In our case to open up to our visitors' strengths and potential. The prologue continues with a pre-show with a few sentences encapsulating The Human Safety Net beliefs and vision: "As human beings, we are full of potential. We all have hopes and dreams." "Yet we are all vulnerable when faced with life's circumstances. What if we looked at each other's potential? What if we supported each other as we grow?"

Orna C. The prologue is like an opera *overture* laying out the key plot elements explored later on in the performance.
Act One is about the power of human potential. The visitors will explore a selection of the twenty-four character strengths related to social entrepreneurship. Visitors can test their perseverance or curiosity, play with their creativity and social intelligence, and have the opportunity to grasp the importance of bravery and reflect on gratitude. Through a personalised form, visitors start to discover what their top strength is.
Act Two is about the power of collaboration. About our capacity to collaborate, to appreciate each other, and achieve goals together. To address this topic we chose to develop only one rather sophisticated and innovative installation. Visitors are invited to collaborate in order to create a beautiful and poetic event. Ico and his team created a wonderful installation, that will certainly have a "wow effect." In Act Two the self-assessment continues with a reflection on strengths like teamwork, leadership, and vision.
Act Three is about the power of social engagement. The power of people helping people. Visitors will discover their top strength, and as said, will be matched with one of the protagonists of The Human Safety Net with similar character strengths. The narrative will therefore be delivered by that same person who will explain the circumstances where that top strength proved important to overcome a social challenge. For example, there is a wonderful story of a refugee who created his cleaning company and who now not only makes a living out of it but is also hiring other people. He describes the challenges and risks he had to face to set up a social enterprise in a foreign country, and how The Human Safety Net provided support in order to acquire the necessary management and administrative skills. He also explains how, in order to succeed on that journey, perseverance—which he learned from his mother—proved key. It is an intimate story. The videos are

Orna C. very short and present very diverse and touching stories. Curious visitors have the opportunity to discover further stories by other protagonists by staying a little longer in Act Three.

In the last part, the Epilogue, the focus is on The Human Safety Net itself, with its scope, field of action, programmes, and partners. But this section is not only about self-promotion: visitors are invited to actively participate: they can take a photo against a background with the name of their top strength or they can choose to donate a small percentage of their ticket price to a specific country. This section is also where visitors collect their exhibition souvenirs: the photos, drawings, writings they made throughout the itinerary. They are also invited to remain connected to The Human Safety Net, as social-media followers or—best case scenario—as social activists.

Ico M. We have dealt with a number of museum and exhibition projects where the goal was not to exhibit objects, but to communicate content, build relationships, and convey concepts and knowledge. This was the case of the Intesa Sanpaolo Savings Museum in Turin, for instance, which explores the meaning and value of saving money.

At The Human Safety Net headquarters, we worked to express the concepts underlying the itinerary as a set of experiences. But we wanted to go further: every feature of the headquarters, from exhibition signage to graphics, from videos to furnishings and accessories, was conceived so as to reflect the same spirit of inclusion, acceptance, and dialogue. In doing so, we singled out three elements that represent the common thread of the project, three elements that also have a strong symbolic function: the first element are tables. We have designed many for this space: tables are archetypal objects, a symbol of sharing, around which people sit to talk, and to meet. The second element are nests, a symbol of hospitality and connection echoed in the structures of the bookcases, which also visually connect the convivial and working spaces. The last element are mirrors,

Ico M. objects with somewhat magical qualities, that in Venice are the expression of a centuries-old tradition. Mirrors are recurring elements in this project, in the cafeteria furnishings and in several installations: allegorical symbols of external beauty, as well as of self-awareness, reflection, and conscience.
For instance, during the last part of the itinerary, in an installation illustrating The Human Safety Net activities, people can take a seat at a table and find a mirror in front of them, in which they see their reflection. But then suddenly the image changes and the face of one of the people involved in the Foundation's projects appears telling their story in a few minutes, saying how they operate, where they work, and what can be done to support them.
Tables, nests, and mirrors are the backbone of our project, a sort of media through which visitors get to know The Human Safety Net experience.

Luca M. This was going to be my next question. You wanted to translate those three symbols into a physical space.

Ico M. Besides the common thread of the recurring symbols (tables, nests, and mirrors), there is also the allegory of the Venetian theatre, stemming from an idea of Davide Rampello, who is in charge of the overall artistic management of the Generali Group project. At the beginning of their exhibition experience, visitors meet in front of a small theatre, a digital diorama with dynamic sets representing Venice, against which they see three real moving puppets, beautifully crafted by the Colla puppet manufacturers. The puppets, which represent three Venetian masks (Harlequin, Columbine, and Pantaloon), are animated by a complex technology and address visitors first in Venetian dialect and then, following a personal interaction, in the visitor's native language. Their presence seems to be suspended in time, between history and fantasy, and running on avant-garde technology. This is an excellent example of how we understand the role of technology within the framework of this project: as a very powerful, yet hidden tool, used to evoke a sense of wonder, to awaken our senses, curiosity and attention.

Luca M. And how did you do this? You said that you needed to approach the exhibition space and the other areas in a coherent way that would shape the top-floor community, which is the real innovative element of the regeneration project carried out by Chipperfield. The third floor did not exist before.

Ico M. We designed these headquarters adopting the same set of codes in all its spaces. The creation of harmonic spaces is part of our research: each room has a distinct format, but they all echo the regular pattern of the architecture's arches and *oculi* series. Harmony between all parts was key towards the creation of the nest area that, in our opinion, encapsulates the new concept of welcome The Human Safety Net promotes. First of all, The Human Safety Net's home is a place where one feels welcome and protected.
The nest idea, which is the main theme of the project, is emphasised by elements such as the copper bookcases, with light inserts and wooden shelves, which also visually recall the intertwining of a nest.
This is what I mean when I speak of environmental design: the interior design is like a flexible device, which conforms to the context and establishes a dialogue; it's something that transcends the physical and plastic concept of design.

Luca M. It's a brand-new place where the community can meet and that is also home to The Human Safety Net. How did you envision the general layout while working on this project?

Ico M. Our project spreads across the entire third floor of the Procuratie Vecchie, which is the actual "home" of The Human Safety Net.
We have imagined it as a welcoming, inviting place, where any visitor can enter, embark on the journey, and learn something about themselves, about others, as well as the Foundation. In short, a place to broaden their gaze. But we have also included operational, work, and conversation spaces, such as areas for co-working and events, and socialising areas such as cafés and terraces.
We conceived the venue as a mix of different functions, with a compositional continuity respectful of the context and designed by the light. The furnishings and partitions overlap the structures without overwhelming or permanently affecting them, enhancing the subdivision of the volumes and the arch sequence lining the floor.

Luca M. How do you expect people will react to your work?
I know that you've worked extensively on this exhibition and its concepts, and that after the opening, people will react in a completely different way... which for me is the most interesting aspect. I learn a lot from people.
So, what are your expectations? Because this exhibition is a challenge, in a way. It's always complex to work with high values, and you also decided to offer a physical experience, after two years of pandemic.
So I imagine people will react differently from how they would have done two years ago. What do you expect?

Orna C. Evaluations are very helpful to better understand the visitors' motivation and their takeaway from the exhibition experience. We usually observe how our visitors use exhibits and we interview them to learn more about what they found inspiring. Six or twelve months later our evaluators call them, because it's important to know what of the exhibition has remained with them. We can certainly discover a wide range of behaviours while they are interacting with the exhibition, but surprisingly the takeaway and impact very often coincide.
Venice, as we all know, is a very touristic city. So we assume that the majority of the visitors will be tourists with totally different backgrounds, motivations and timeframes. To tackle this diversity, our evaluation is based on John H. Falk's research. Falk is one of the greatest experts when it comes to the evaluation of visitor behaviour and he divides visitors into eight different categories. In The Human Safety Net exhibition I figure we will have three main typologies:
The "experience seekers": their motivation is primarily the experience itself. They want to play and interact with others, feel happy when they discover more about themselves and might be interested in finding out more about The Human Safety Net.
The "explorers": they are really interested in the topic of social engagement and want to understand The Human Safety Net's approach and impact. They will certainly stay longer in order to take a deep dive into the exhibition.
The "generally interested": this is not one of Falk's categories, but we might have many visitors who are attracted by the Procuratie Vecchie building with its history, architecture and restoration. The exhibition is not their focus, but we might succeed in capturing their interest.
Regarding the two years of the pandemic: from our *Dialogue Exhibitions* operation across different countries we have learnt that as soon as the pandemic threat retreats people really crave for social and cultural events. It is a sort of counter effect following the isolation, lockdown, and curfew

It is a sort of counter effect following the isolation, lockdown, and curfew experiences. The human need and urgency to share time and experiences together is strong and vibrant.

Orna C. experiences. The human need and urgency to share time and experiences together is strong and vibrant. I expect The Human Safety Net exhibition will rapidly attract visitors precisely because of its innovative and interactive nature. Furthermore, its content is very timely, since especially during the pandemic we became aware of our own vulnerability and had to rely on our strengths and solidarity. And that's exactly the point of The Human Safety Net.

Ico M. Our projects are based on the reactions and operate on the behaviour of the people who use them. In this sense, we believe that besides a three-dimensional space, the fourth, time-related dimension is also fundamental: therefore we meticulously regulate the relationship of our visitors with the time they spend in the exhibition, learning and interacting. And this is the approach we used in this new The Human Safety Net home in Venice, in the exhibition itinerary, as well as in other reception and work spaces; each action has its own rhythm, and we have designed the spaces according to the pace that visitors will set based on their personal needs. Looking, reading, listening, surprises, and reflections all combine forming something of a perfect tempo.

Looking, reading, listening, surprises, and reflections all combine forming something of a perfect tempo.

I would also address the theme of context, which here plays a key role. One of the most interesting features of the project is its multi-faceted link with Venice. We have devoted considerable attention to the context. Venice has a unique nature, and it is a city that has also been able to welcome cultures from all over the world. From The Human Safety Net's headquarters in the Procuratie Vecchie, visitors will have the chance to enjoy a view of Venice, as well as a historical overview of the city.
Throughout the exhibition itinerary, visitors will always feel connected to the surroundings through the *oculi*, the peculiar round windows running along the facades of the entire floor. In some of them, the view has been enhanced through a technological magnification system which, like the optical devices Canaletto used, allows visitors to explore the opposite side of St. Mark's Square. There is also an installation that acts as a "time telescope," allowing people to take a three-dimensional look at a number of Venice landmarks (Giudecca, Rialto Bridge, Arsenale, Burano, and Murano) as they were in the sixteenth century. There has been much discussion with Davide Rampello about the idea of linking the exhibition with the territory, that we both consider as central.
The connection with Venice is also referenced in the choice of materials used to create the furnishings —wood, ropes, glass, copper, and mirrors—, designed by our studio for the reception and cafeteria areas. In their material quality they also evoke the spirit of craftsmanship: handmade items that are typical of Venice and its territory. For instance, the characteristic Venetian *bricole* (the oak wooden posts used in the lagoon to mark navigable routes) represent the load-bearing components for an installation of the exhibition itinerary, devoted to teamwork in Act Two. It's a sort of water section of the lagoon, crystallised and supported by *bricole*, where you can take a deep dive into an active and collective experience. The organic wood benches in the café recall those of the historic Venetian cafés. Even the patterns of the rugs, placed in various rooms, hark back to Venetian motifs, such as the Palazzo Ducale decorated arches or the glass *millefiori murrine*. In short, Venice is an indispensable and pivotal facet of this new The Human Safety Net headquarters and of the experience its visitors will enjoy there.

BIOGRAPHIES

Simon Anholt is a policy advisor, author and researcher who has provided global leadership and innovation in the public, private and non-profit sectors. He is publisher of the *Good Country Index*, and his TED talk launching the first edition of the study is the all-time most viewed TED talk about government, with twelve million views. Anholt has advised the heads of State and heads of government of sixty countries, helping them engage more ethically, imaginatively and strategically with the international community (including for example Bhutan's groundbreaking *Gross National Happiness* initiative and the widely imitated *StartUp Chile* programme). His original work on measuring and managing the images of countries has developed into a global industry. This work has been supported since 2005 by the Anholt-Ipsos Nation Brands Index, a research framework which has accumulated over a billion datapoints.

Diana Bagnoli, is a photojournalist from Turin; she studied photography in Barcelona, where she began to explore portraits and reportage, taking an interest in social issues and documenting the colourful humanity surrounding her. In 2009, she was "Photographer of the Year" at the FIOF Photography Awards; since then, she has been working as a storyteller, with a special focus on the diverse facets of society, giving voice to marginal groups and looking for new and topical life stories. Between 2015 and 2019 she carried out projects on mystics around the world and documented their indigenous cultures. Bagnoli recently received the COVID-19 Emergency Fund from the National Geographic Society, to document the work of the Cuban Doctors Brigade in Italy, and an honourable mention at the IPA Awards and the World Water Day Photo Contest. She has collaborated with several NGOs, including Amref Health Africa and NPH in Haiti. Her work has been published in international magazines including *GEO Magazine*, *The Guardian*, *The Washington Post*, *National Geographic*, and *Elle*. Her work has been exhibited internationally, at the Visa Pour L'Image 2020 in France, at the Indian Photo Festival in New Delhi, and at the 2019 Ethical Photography Festival in Lodi, Beijing, and Sydney.

Simone Bemporad, journalist and then business executive, has worked in the communication and institutional relations for companies such as IRI (Istituto italiano per la Ricostruzione Industriale), Enel, Finmeccanica-Leonardo and, since 2014, Assicurazioni Generali. For Generali, he launched The Human Safety Net, now active in over twenty countries around the world, and the Procuratie Vecchie restoration project. of the integration of Sustainability into Generali's business strategy. On this subject with Renata Codello he co-authored *Imprese private e pubbliche virtù* (Marsilio Editori, 2022, preface by Romano Prodi). Italian and US citizen, he is adjunct fellow at the Centre for Strategic and International Studies in Washington, DC.

Cesare Benelli was born in Tuscany, in his grandfather's small hotel in Montecatini. His first memories are linked to the guests and to the eels his mother, the only Venetian in an otherwise all-Tuscan family, used to cook. Aged two he moved to Venice Lido, where his maternal grandfather opened the Trattoria Toscana. After briefly undertaking Pharmacy studies, Cesare started running restaurant businesses on the beach and travelling during the winter. In the late 1970s he moved to Austin, Texas, to work in a large hotel chain. Here he met Diane, who was to become his wife and "accomplice." Back in Venice, they opened Al Covo. Cesare has a clear-cut vision of catering to serve food celebrating local ingredients and products, a formula that still works beautifully for his restaurant and his Venetian colleagues with whom he created the "Associazione dei Ristoranti della Buona Accoglienza."

Cristiano Billia was born in Trieste in 1972 and studied Architecture at the Istituto Universitario di Architettura in Venice (IUAV). He has worked for David Chipperfield Architects since 2002, firstly in London and since 2008 in Milan, becoming Associate in 2010 and Associate Director in 2016. In over 20 years' experience, he has led commercial, cultural, residential projects and numerous competitions. He has led the development of store concepts for fashion brands, as well as concept stores for multibrand retailers. He has also led the realisation of projects for the San Michele Cemetery in Venice, the Mudec – Museum of Cultures in Milan and the Procuratie Vecchie in Venice. Along with other projects, he is currently leading the conversion of the Caserma Piave for the University of Padua.

Arthur C. Brooks is the William Henry Bloomberg Professor of the Practice of Public Leadership at Harvard Kennedy School and Professor of Management Practice at Harvard Business School. Before joining the Harvard faculty in July of 2019, he served for ten years as president of the American Enterprise Institute (AEI), a public policy think tank in Washington, DC. Brooks is the author of twelve books, including the national bestsellers *Love Your Enemies* (Northampton, MA, Broadside Books, 2019) and *The Conservative Heart* (Northampton, MA, Broadside Books, 2015), and *From Strength to Strength* (London, Portfolio, 2022). He has also published dozens of academic journal articles and the textbook *Social Entrepreneurship* (2008). He is a columnist for *The Atlantic*, host of the podcast *How to Build a Happy Life*, and subject of the 2019 documentary film *The Pursuit*, which *Variety* in August 2019 named as one of the best documentaries on Netflix. He gives more than one hundred speeches per year around the U.S., Europe, and Asia.

David Chipperfield was born in London in 1953 and studied architecture at the Kingston School of Art and the Architectural Association School of Architecture in London before working in the practices of Douglas Stephen, Richard Rogers and Norman Foster. In 1985 he founded David Chipperfield Architects, which today has over three hundred staff at its offices in London, Berlin, Milan and Shanghai. David Chipperfield has taught and held conferences in Europe and the United States, and has received honorary degrees from the universities of Kingston and Kent. He is a member of the Royal Institute of British Architects (RIBA) and an honorary fellow of both the American Institute of Architects (AIA) and the Bund Deutscher Architekten (BDA). In 2009 he was awarded the Order of Merit of the Federal Republic of Germany and in 2010 he received a knighthood for services to architecture in the UK and Germany. In 2011 he received the RIBA Royal Gold Medal for Architecture and in 2013 the Praemium Imperiale from the Japan Art Association, while in 2021 he was appointed member of the Order of the Companions of Honour in recognition of a lifetime's work. In 2012 he curated the Venice Biennale thirteenth International Architecture Exhibition and in 2020 he was the guest editor of the Italian magazine *Domus*.

Renata Codello, PhD in Italy and UK, is an architect. Former manager at the Ministry of Culture, she was Superintendent in Venice and Rome; director of the MiBACT Regional secretariat for Veneto and Friuli Venezia Giulia, she is now the general secretary of the Giorgio Cini Foundation, Venice.
Expert in restoration and management of cultural heritage, she was a professor at the Faculty of Architecture in Genoa and at the Faculty of Engineering of the Tor Vergata University, Rome. She also worked at the Ca' Foscari University and currently teaches Restoration at the IUAV. She restored the works of Carlo Scarpa in Venice. In the Lagoon city, she also designed and realised the new headquarters of the Accademia di Belle Arti, located in the sixteenth-century complex of the Ospedale degli Incurabili alle Zattere (1998–2004) and, with Tobia Scarpa, she planned and supervised the works for the expansion of the Gallerie dell'Accademia (1999–2014).
From 2013 to 2018, she was a member of the Royal Institute of British Architects.
She collaborated with Tadao Ando for the restoration of Punta della Dogana; from 2000 to 2015, she directed several contemporary architectural projects in Venice.
Author of books and essays on restoration and architecture, she is advisor to the Italian Presidency of the Republic and superior advisor of the Bank of Italy; for her merits, she was awarded Commander of the Italian Republic.

Orna Cohen is the co-founder of Dialogue Social Enterprise. Exhibitions, in her understanding, are drivers for transformation and must tackle the most pressing of social challenges: the inclusion of marginalised communities. As a result, Orna's exhibitions such as *Dialogue in the Dark* or *Dialogue in Silence* foster empathy globally, and provide jobs for disadvantaged or disabled individuals. Before founding the Dialogue Social Enterprise, Orna created the renowned *Cité des Enfants*, an interactive exhibition for children at La Cité des Sciences in Paris. Orna was named Chevalier de l'ordre des Arts et des Lettres by the French government to acknowledge her contribution to science and technology education.

Guido Guidi was born in Cesena in 1941. His research focuses on contemporary landscape transformation. Among his works, worth mentioning are his series on the spontaneous architectures in eastern Romagna (1971–1972), on the landscape of the Romea Road (1975–1990), on the industrial areas of Porto Marghera and Ravenna (1983–1997), and on the "inserted" landscapes along the Napoleonic Road (1993–1996). These projects have been showcased in a number of international exhibitions and published in the related catalogues, including: Venice Biennale (2006, 2009, 2011, and 2013 editions), Mendrisio Architecture Academy 2013, ICCD Rome 2013, Wolsburg 2007, CCB Lisbon 2014, Huis Marseille 2014, Musée de la Ville de Paris 2018, CCA (1999, 2002, and 2009), Whitney Museum 2001, and MCA Chicago 2002. Guidi has published several monographs, including *5 Viaggi 1990–1998*, 2021; *Tra l'altro, 1976–81*, 2020; *Lunario, 1968–1999*, 2020; *In Veneto, 1984–89*, 2019; *In Sardegna, 1974–2011*, 2019; *Per Strada*, 2018; *Dietro casa*, 2018; *Guardando a Est*, 2015; *The Interview Issue*, *Aperture* 220, n. 50/63, 2015; *Veramente*, 2014; *Preganziol 1983*, 2013; *Cinque paesaggi, 1983–1993*, 2013; *La Figura dell'Orante*, 2012; *A New Map of Italy*, 2011; *Carlo Scarpa's Tomba Brion*, 2011; *Fiume*, 2010; *VOL I*, 2006; *Bunker Along the Atlantic Wall*, 2006; *PK TAV 139+500*, 2006; *Rimini Atlas*, pTcp 2006; *La lunga posa*, 2006; *Guido Guidi 1969–2004*, 2004; *In Between Cities*, 2003; *SS9*, 2000; *InaCasa;* 1999. *Gardenia*; 1997; *Rimini Nord*, 1991; *Lo spazio della quiete*, 1983; *Guido Guidi,* 1983. In 1995, *Guido Guidi, Varianti* won the title of Italy's best photography book of the year.

Andrew Hopkins, Professor and Chair of Architectural History at the University of L'Aquila, was previously Assistant Director of the British School in Rome. Part of his PhD (Courtauld Institute London, 1995) on Venetian architecture was awarded the Essay Medal of 1996 by the Society of Architectural Historians (GB). Andrew was a Fellow at Harvard University's Center for Italian Renaissance Studies at Villa I Tatti in Florence in 2003–2004; Paul Mellon Senior Visiting Fellow, Centre for Advanced Studies in the Visual Arts, National Gallery of Art, Washington D.C. in 2009; Getty Research Institute Fellow 2013 and Beaufort Fellow, St. John's College Cambridge 2014. Among his many publications: *Santa Maria della Salute: Architecture and Ceremony in Baroque Venice* (Cambridge University Press, 2000); *Italian Architecture from Michelangelo to Borromini* (Thames and Hudson, 2002); with Arnold Witte, *Alois Riegl, The Origins of Baroque Art in Rome*, (Los Angeles, Getty Publications, 2010); *Baldassare Longhena and Venetian Baroque Architecture* (revised edition in English Yale University Press, 2012); *La città del Seicento* (Bari, Laterza 2014).

Michel Lussault, born January 29th 1960, he is a geographer, and full professor of urban global studies in the University of Lyon, (Ecole Normale Supérieure), France. Well-known French specialist in urban studies and theoretical geography, he has published, since 1990, many books and scientific papers. He gave many lectures in universities in France and in other countries. Since 2005 his research has focused on study of global urbanisation as a new "milieu" for inhabitants and on the issue of urban vulnerability in an anthropocenic world. Since 2010 he's addressing the topic of "spatial care" as a new way of thinking global change adaptation and the topic of urban anthropocene.

Aldo Mazzocco was born in Harare, Zimbabwe, on 2 September 1961, is married with three children and lives in Padua.
From March 2021 has been appointed Head of Private Markets and Real Assets, continuing to maintain his role as Chief Executive Officer and General Manager of Generali Real Estate S.p.A. and Chairman of Citylife S.p.A., from May 2017. From March 2018 has been appointed President of Generali Real Estate SGR S.p.A.
He has been Head of Real Estate at Cassa Depositi e Prestiti, President of CDP Immobiliare and President of CDP Investimenti SGR.
From 2011 to May 2017 he has been President of Assoimmobiliare. He has been CEO of Beni Stabili SIIQ from 2001 to 2015 and Directeur Général Délégué of Foncière des Régions from 2011 to 2015; President of Beni Stabili Gestioni SGR; Chairman of the Board of Management of Investire Immobiliare SGR; Member of the Board of Management of Beni Stabili Gestioni SGR; Board member at IM.SER; on the Board of Beni Stabili Development Milano Greenway; Member of the Board of EPRA – European Public Real Estate Association – Brussels; on the Board of Beni Stabili Property Service.
Up to 2015 he was a member of the Management Committee of Assonime. He is currently member of the Royal Institution of Chartered Surveyors. He has also been Member of Directoire di Foncière des Régions S.A. – Paris, Managing Director of C.F.I. and Director General of G. Pivato.
He graduated in Civil Engineering at the University of Padua and obtained a Master's Degree in Business Administration from the Bocconi School of Management, Milan.

Ico Migliore, a three-time Compasso d'Oro Award winner, teaches at the Design School of the Polytechnic University of Milan and is Chair Professor at the Dongseo University of Busan (South Korea). With Mara Servetto he has co-founded Migliore+Servetto Architects and designed several major international destinations such as the Chopin Museum in Warsaw, the permanent exhibition at the ADI Design Museum in Milan, and the logo, identity and special set-ups of the Egyptian Museum in Turin. He has created the Blue Line Park in Busan (South Korea), involving the transformation of five kilometres of disused waterfront railway into a linear park, as well as the Max Mara Coats travelling exhibition that has been set up in Berlin, Tokyo, Beijing, Moscow and Seoul.
He has contributed to the discourse on interior and exhibition design with articles and books, including *Spacemorphing* (Milan, Five Continents, 2007), *Time to Exhibit* (Milan, Franco Angeli, 2019), and *Sketches, Maps, Sceneries* (Milan, Electa, 2021).

Luca Molinari, born in Lodi in 1966 is an architect, art critic, curator, and Full Professor of Theory and Architectural Design at the Luigi Vanvitelli University of Campania. He is an active part of the special projects organised by the Marsilio group and since 2020 he has been Scientific Director of the M9 museum in Mestre, as well as Scientific Manager for the architectural features of the Milan Triennale (2001–2004). In 2010 he curated *Ailati. Riflessi dal futuro*, the Italian Pavilion at the Venice Biennale twelfth International Architecture Exhibition. His most recent publications include *Le case che siamo* (Milan, Nottetempo, 2016), and *Dismisura. La teoria e il progetto per l'architettura italiana* (Milan, Skira, 2019).

Guadalupe Nettel was born in Mexico City in 1973. She is the author of four collections of short stories, including *Bezoar: And Other Unsettling Stories* (2020) and *Natural Histories: Stories*

(2014), and of four novels, among which *Still-Born* (2022). She has received several awards, including the Franco-Mexican Antonin Artaud Prize (2008), the German Anna Seghers Prize (2009) and the Ribera del Duero Short Fiction Prize (2013). Most of her work has been translated into English and Italian.

Itai Palti, born in Tel Aviv, Israel in 1983, is a practising architect and researcher focusing on designing with the human experience in mind. He directs Hume, a science-informed architecture and urban design practice backed by research at the Human Metrics Lab. In 2015, Itai founded the Conscious Cities movement: a new field of research and practice for the creation of aware and responsive people-centred environments based on data analysis, AI, tech, and behavioural science in design. Itai is director of the Centre for Conscious Design, a think tank focused on using design to address society's present and future urban challenges.

Paolo Pejrone (Turin, 1941) was a pupil of Russell Page and Roberto Burle Marx. Since 1970, he has been working as garden designer in Italy, France, Switzerland, Saudi Arabia, Greece, England, Germany, Spain, Belgium, Monaco, and Austria. The numerous public and private gardens that he has designed include: the green areas of the Pitrizza hotel in Costa Smeralda, the Istituto Bancario San Paolo Turin, the Hotel Excelsior in Venice, the Four Seasons and Principe di Savoia hotels in Milan, the Banca Popolare di Lodi in Turin, the Garden of the Basilica of the Holy Cross in Jerusalem, Rome, the Furla plant in Bologna, the Hotel Pellicano in Porto Ercole, the PKB Privatbank branch in Lugano, Switzerland, the Sassi station in Turin, the Gallery of Modern Art in Turin, and the Touffou Castle in Poitiers, France; Pejrone also designed the gardens of the municipalities of Villar Perosa (Turin), Cavallermaggiore (Cuneo), Parma, Saluzzo (Cuneo), Savigliano (Cuneo) and Offenburg, Germany. He is the author of several books about gardening, and his latest is *I dubbi del giardiniere* (Milan, Einaudi, 2021).

Davide Rampello is a curator, artistic director, manager, and cultural consultant. Over the years, he has been the promoter of important exhibitions in various venues such as the Biennale and the Gallerie dell'Accademia in Venice and has overseen the artistic direction of national and international cultural events such as the Carnival of Venice, the Italian Pavilion at the Shanghai Expo 2010, the Zero Pavilion at the 2015 Milan Expo, and the Italian Pavilion at the Expo 2021 Dubai. From 2003 to 2011 he was president of the Milan Triennale. He is currently the creative director of Rampello & Partners, a company whose main activity involves producing exhibitions, events, and cultural communication projects. In the academic field, he has taught and still teaches courses on artistic and cultural events planning , as well as on the enhancement of the territory, at the universities of Padua, IULM, and the Polytechnic University of Milan.

Adele Re Rebaudengo, born in Turin but Venetian by adoption, she graduated in Law; after having worked as a lawyer for a few years, she devoted herself to theatre and then to photography, promoting, creating, and curating numerous festivals, exhibitions, and art publications with the greatest masters of international photography, in collaboration with museums and institutions.
President of the Venice Gardens Foundation since 2014, she promotes and implements projects aimed at the restoration and protection of parks, gardens, and valuable historical and artistic assets, as well as enhancing the fundamental role that these places play in a social and community context, favouring the harmonious interaction between spirit and nature. In pursuit of these goals, she carried out the renovation of the Royal Gardens of Venice, and is currently engaged in the restoration and conservation of the garden of Palladio's convent of the Santissimo Redentore, a place of the highest historical and spiritual value.

Alberto Toso Fei descends from an ancient family of Murano glassmakers, that has been living in Venice since 1351. Journalist, writer, and essayist, his works have been translated into several languages. His books on the secret and legendary history of Venice, inspired by his interest in oral traditions, have become theatrical performances, works of art, installations, treasure hunts, and tourist itineraries. Like a living time machine, with his storytelling he creates recitals, conferences-shows, TEDx talks, activities, and online events, which he also shares on social networks. He is a leading figure in the cultural scene of Venice, and a well-versed scholar on the history of the city.

Emma Ursich is Generali's Group Head of Corporate Identity and Executive Officer of The Human Safety Net Foundation. A graduate in Oriental Studies from the University of Oxford, she has been working in reputation management, development of cultural iniatives, stakeholder and community engagement for over twenty years. In her work she follows the belief that reputation depends on consistently bringing to life an organisation's purpose. This has led her to reorganise the Group's strategic philanthropy with The Human Safety Net, initiating programmes tackling some of the key socio-demographic issues of our times, such as social mobility and migration. In Venice, Emma has worked closely with architects and curators to create a new hub for social innovation inside the Procuratie Vecchie, mobilising experts, NGOs and the community.

Giuseppe Zampieri was born in Vicenza in 1967 and after graduating in architecture from the Istituto Universitario di Architettura di Venezia (IUAV), in 1996 he joined David Chipperfield Architects, first in London and then in Milan from 2006, initially as Managing Director and Design Director and then as partner from 2016. Over twenty-five years he has directed an extensive array of national and international projects and a series of works that have won both national and international competitions including, in Italy, the historic Centre of Salerno, the San Michele Cemetery in Venice, the Palace of Justice in Salerno, the Cultural Hub in Verona, the Mudec – Museum of Cultures in Milan, the Castello Sforzesco in Milan, the Complex of Santa Chiara in Pisa, the Campus of the University of Padua. In the last fifteen years, he has driven the development of store concepts for Monobrands as well as concept stores and store concepts for Multibrands and curated the design of the exhibitions dedicated to David Chipperfield Architects at Palazzo della Ragione in Padua, Arsenali Medicei in Pisa and at the Basilica Palladiana in Vicenza. He directed the Procuratie Vecchie renovation in Venice and is currently working on Palazzo Ancilotto in Treviso and Caserma Piave in Padua.

ASSICURAZIONI GENERALI

Group CEO
Philippe Donnet

The Concept
Simone Bemporad
Emma Ursich

Restoration Project Commissioner
Generali Real Estate

CEO
Aldo Mazzocco

Project Team
Rocco Antoniello
Fabio Floridan
Riccardo Guzzi
Paolo Micucci

Competition Management
GSS PROCUREMENT
Antonio Pollice
Alessandra Totaro
Massimo Zicari

Legal Team
Silvia Bardusco
Pierluigi Martino
Anna Oneto

Owner
Generali Italia

Country Manager, CEO of Generali Italia and Global Business Lines
Marco Sesana

Architectonic Project
DAVID CHIPPERFIELD ARCHITECTS Srl, Milan

Partners
David Chipperfield
Giuseppe Zampieri

Associate Director
Cristiano Billia

Associates
Adolfo Berardozzi, Andrea Cocco, Carlo Zucchia

Project Team
Simone Diego Alessi, Federica Amoruso, Thomas Benk, Corrado Bongiorno, Cecilia Bottoni, Niccolò Brussa, Teresa Cancellari, Marta Capacciola, Filippo Carcano, Francesca Carino, Carlo Federico Cattò, Fabiano Cocozza, Maria Elena Codazzi, Paolo Dell'Elce, Stefano Goffi, Tsukasa Goto, Samuel Lodetti, Eugenio Matteazzi, Tommaso Meena, Daniel Mira García, Sofia Nobis, Brigid O'Donnell, Stefano Penazzi, Matthijs Sioen, Tiziana Staffieri, Davide Tassera, Federico Turelli, Wouter Verstraete, Maria Chiara Virgili

Competition Team
Cosmin Amato, Pietro Bagnoli, Corrado Bongiorno, Cecilia Bottoni, Filippo Carcano, Carlo Federico Cattò, Tommaso Certo, Fabiano Cocozza, Maria Elena Codazzi, Federica Corrà, Paolo Dell'Elce, Tsukasa Goto, Nicola Guercilena, Seunggeun Jee, Chiara Lippi, Eugenio Matteazzi, Gabriele Pagani, Paolo Volpetti, Federica Zerbo

In collaboration with
DAVID CHIPPERFIELD ARCHITECTS, Berlin
Thomas Benk, Anke Fritzsch, Christopher Jonas

Quantity Surveyor
GAD Srl, Milan
Gianpiero Aresi, Luca Cedrelli, Francesco Minoia

Executive Architects
ZERO4UNO INGEGNERIA Srl, Venezia
Romeo Scarpa

FRANCO GAZZARRI ARCHITETTO, Mestre

TA ARCHITETTURA, Mestre
Diego Boldo, Giulia Conti, Anna Lisa Girolami, Alberto Torsello

Project Coordination
ARTELIA, Milan
Giorgio Alberti, Giuseppe Baudille, Matteo Lavazza, Marco Paolacci, Massimo Vedovato

Structural Engineer
ARUP, Milan
Federico Bormetti, Luca Buzzoni, Guglielmo Carra, Giammichele Melis

Services Engineer
ARUP, Milan
Paolo Bianchi, Paolo Cresci

Acoustic Consultant
MANENS TIFS, Verona
Marco Trame, Roberto Zecchin

Fire Consultant
STUDIO MISTRETTA, Milan
Valentina Liggi, Silvestre Mistretta

Facade Consultant
ARUP, Milan

Lighting Consultant
VIABIZZUNO Srl, Bentivoglio (Bologna)
Giacomo Coppe, Francesco Finetti, Mario Nanni, Giulia Pulga

Works Management
TA ARCHITETTURA
Diego Boldo, Giulia Conti, Marta Corder, Anna Girolami, Alberto Torsello, Andrea Zanchettin

General Contractor
RIZZANI DE ECCHER Spa, Pozzuolo del Friuli (Udine)

Contracting Firms
Attia Group Srl
Badoer Infissi Srl
Barausse Srl a socio unico
Boscolo "Bielo" Ivano Srl
Braga Spa
Brera 89 Srl
Brugnotto Srl
C.N.C. Consorzio Nazionale Costruttori
Carpenterie Tessari Srl
Decomar di Stradella Omar
E.D.L. Costruzioni Srl
Edilmar Srl
Edilnoleggi Valente & Partners SCArL
Elettromeccanica Trevigiana Snc
Ettore Bertoldini Costruzioni Metalliche
Europavimenti Sas di Morelli Salvatore
Falegnameria Baradel Srl
Fiel Spa
Fime Di Persello Srl
F.R. Engineering Srl
F.lli Gobbetto Snc
Gdm Lattonerie Girotto Srl
Gr Strutture Srl
L.B.M. Bettella L. e C. Srl
Lithos Srl
Mgn Srl
Margraf Spa
Marson Srl
Resimix Srl
Restauri D'arte Snc di Sernagiotto E.
Tecnoelettra Srl
Twincad Srl
Vergati Srl
Viabizzuno Srl

Content Design
Programme Management
Maria Elena Bruno de Curtis
Deborah Zamaro

Venice Hub
Gloria Bondi
Alexia Boro
Elisabetta Randazzo

The Human Safety Net Team
Alessandra Aquilani, Alan Barbieri, Lisa Batani Irene Candian, Yves Carbonnelle, Patrick Hoffmann, Francesca Monti, Antonio Palmiero, Arthur Reverchon, Maria Teresa Ricciardi, Stefano Rovelli, Kate Sullivan, Marta Zanetti

Art Direction
RAMPELLO & PARTNERS, Milan
Art Director
Davide Rampello
Creative Content & Project Manager
Greta Carandini

Exhibition Curators
DIALOGUE SOCIAL ENTERPRISE, Hamburg
Orna Cohen and Andreas Heinecke, curators

Project Team
Programme, Interactive Exhibits & Texts
Annkatrin Meyer
Noémie Sei

With the Expertise of
MAYERSON ACADEMY, Cincinnati
Karen Graves, Jillian Coppley

Jasper Visser

Editorial Consulting
Aaron Maines, English
Luca Masia, Italian

Interior, Exhibition and Multimedia Design
Creative Direction
Ico Migliore
Mara Servetto

Migliore+Servetto Team
Coordination & Project Leaders
Daniele Pellizzoni
Francesca Rapisarda
and
Giorgia Borroni
Maddalena Guglielmelli

with
Giovanni Bettinelli
Lucia Carughi
Rossella Forioli
Federica Galbusieri
Giacomo Lietti
Riccardo Mara
Guido Mollica
Francesco Russo
Maria Elena Vona
Zhen Yuan

Illustrations of Exhibit n. 11
Michele Tranquillini

Venice Theatre Puppets
Atelier Colla

Set-up
ARCO Srl, Furniture
ETT Spa, Technology and Software
Gruppo Fallani Srl, Furniture for the exhibition space

Technical Consultant, Programme Management and Content Design
Roberto Ferraresi
Diego Paccagnella

Exhibition Visitor Analytics
Risposte Turismo
Francesco di Cesare
Anthony La Salandra

User Experience, Exibition Space and Ticket Office Software
Andrea Casadei

Food & Beverage Consultant
Oscar Cavallera

ASSICURAZIONI GENERALI
Alberto Ces
Furio Curri
Lucrezia Ganzitti
Roberto Kovacic
Maria Lorini
Cesare Marsili
Nicola Padovese
Paolo Pitacco
Dalia Pizzocchero
Raimondo Rocco
Nicola Santin
Valerio Venier

THE HUMAN SAFETY NET
Board of Directors
Gabriele Galateri di Genola
Chair Person
Philippe Donnet
Aldo Minucci
Simone Bemporad
Monica Alessandra Possa
Lucia Silva

Audit Committee
Cristina Morgan
Roberto Odierna
Massimo Romano

Executive Officer
Emma Ursich

GENERALI ITALIA
Meris Bagagiolo
David Cis

GENERALI REAL ESTATE
Claudia Ansoldi
Anna Fanizza
Benedetto Giustiniani
Giovanni Guadagnin

GENERALI BUSINESS SOLUTIONS
Massimo Bandini
Alessandro Brocca
Claudio Caccialanza
Paola Coppa
Roberta Destefani
Alessandro Greco
Cristina Morgan
Massimiliano Pressello
Michele Schiavone
Andrea Xompero
Stefano Zen

GENERALI OPERATIONS SERVICE PLATFORM
Raffaele Bressanutti
Ruggero Forni
Fabio Grilli
Paolo Lizza

Acknowledgements

Venice LAB. Rethinking St. Mark's Square, is the result of a great concerted effort by a number of people who have dealt with the projects discussed in these pages, offering a broad range of insights and points of view.
Assicurazioni Generali, which commissioned this project, would like to thank the publisher Luca De Michelis for the attention he devoted to such a high-profile book on Venice, the city of Marsilio Editori, coinciding with the sixtieth anniversary of the foundation of this prestigious publishing house; the curator of the volume, Luca Molinari, a sensitive architect who was able gain an in-depth vision of the project and make a strong personal contribution to it; and the editor, Martina Mian, for her resilience and cheerful humour, even in the most difficult moments.
Special thanks also go to all the authors who shared their ideas, voiced their opinions, and helped shape an unprecedented dialogue, a meeting point in diversity, as Venice itself is; without forgetting the photographic contribution of a master of the highest level such as Guido Guidi, and the original outlook provided by Diana Bagnoli, a photojournalist.
Furthermore, we are grateful to Philippe Donnet, Generali Group CEO, for his leadership and support in this project, so important for Venice and so symbolic for the company, on the occasion of the one hundred ninetieth anniversary of its foundation; all this led to the restoration of a building and to the revival of the company's mission, with a contemporary and inclusive touch, which resulted in the structure's opening to the public for the first time in its long history; we are also grateful to President Gabriele Galateri of Genola, for his unwavering support as guide of The Human Safety Net Foundation, and to Cristiano Borean, Group Chief Financial Officer of the Generali, for his constant and courageous support at all stages of the project.
The management team of the Generali Group has been an important resource for involving thousands of people around the world and has represented the backbone of the enthusiasm that has brought us here, with such stunning results.
We thank the Ministry of Culture, especially the Ministers Dario Franceschini and Alberto Bonisoli, the Superintendence of Architectural Heritage and Landscape of Venice, specifically architects Emanuela Carpani and Ilaria Cavaggioni, the Municipality of Venice, first and foremost Mayor Luigi Brugnaro, Morris Ceron, Derek Donadini, and all his staff, for their careful guidance and supervision in the restoration and upgrade process.
Special thanks also go to the Prefect of Venice, Vittorio Zappalorto who, with administrative and cultural foresight, as Special Commissioner laid the groundwork for launching the restoration project.
It was an honour and a privilege to work alongside Sir David Chipperfield, Giuseppe Zampieri, Cristiano Billia, and the entire team of David Chipperfield Architects, on a path to a deeper discovery of the core values of the Procuratie Vecchie, revitalised and enhanced with a brilliant spirit for future generations.
We extend our gratitude to the construction supervision, under the sagacious, far-sighted, and passionate supervision of the architect Alberto Torsello, a great Venetian soul, and all his collaborators.
Our gratitude should also be extended to Aldo Mazzocco, CEO of Generali Real Estate, Paolo Micucci, Riccardo Guzzi, Rocco Antoniello, Fabio Floridan, Roberto Ferraresi, and to all the extraordinary team for their vision, professionalism, and courage in successfully completing the work at the Procuratie Vecchie in such challenging times, during the Covid-19 pandemic, and without ever losing heart in the face of many obstacles and unexpected events. Generali Real Estate has sensitively supported and accompanied the vision for a new communal use of the spaces, under the aegis of The Human Safety Net, as well as the entire partnership path for the regeneration of the Royal Gardens.
We thank Marco Sesana, CEO of Generali Italia, the property owner of the Procuratie Vecchie, together with his collaborators, for their teamwork throughout the project cycle and for having breathed new life into the management offices, the heart of the lion company's identity since its inception.
Our gratitude goes to all the companies that have worked on this project, bringing their passion, skills, and expertise, ranging from restoration to the greatest Venetian craftsmanship, to the most advanced technologies, so that we can protect this icon of history and better serve the users of the new spaces.
We are also very thankful to the whole team of The Human Safety Net Foundation, which has passionately followed the development of the new house over the years, starting with Deborah Zamaro and Maria Elena Bruno de Curtis; to Maria Teresa Ricciardi for the sterling professionalism with which she has designed the new structures and processes; to Yves Carbonelle for bringing The Human Safety Net's spirit inside the exhibition; and then to the people who followed the creation of this volume with expertise and care, starting from Gloria Bondi and Arthur Reverchon; to the Programme Team—Alan Barbieri, Kate Sullivan, Stefano Rovelli and Patrick Hoffmann—for their commitment to making The Human Safety Net's mission and programmes an integral part of the content of the Foundation's new home; as well as Lisa Batani, Alessandra Aquilani, Marta Zanetti, Antonio Palmiero, and Elisabetta Randazzo for their unflagging support for the development of the project in all its facets.
The public relations staff of Generali and The Human Safety Net ensured that the project immediately had the visibility it deserves, and which is brought to fruition in this book.
Irene Candian, Roberto Alatri, Sonia Sicco, Laura Basso, and Susanna Tironi, together with their team, provided time and passion to tell a unique story. Mina Maisto in Rome acted as a patient and expert guide in navigating the complex and often urgent institutional and administrative approval procedures.
Additionally, we would like to thank all the following list of employees of Generali Group and GBS, GOSP who worked to make everything go smoothly and come together, even when that was not the case: Claudia Ansoldi, Meris Bagagiolo, Massimo Bandini, Raffaele Bressanutti, Alessandro Brocca, Claudio Caccialanza, Alberto Ces, David Cis, Paola Coppa, Furio Curri, Roberta Destefani, Anna Fanizza, Ruggero Forni, Lucrezia Ganzitti, Benedetto Giustiniani, Alessandro Greco, Fabio Grilli, Giovanni Guadagnin, Roberto Kovacic, Paolo Lizza, Maria Lorini, Cesare Marsili, Cristina Morgan, Nicola Padovese, Paolo Pitacco, Dalia Pizzocchero, Antonio Pollice, Massimiliano Pressello, Raimondo Rocco, Nicola Santin, Michele Schiavone, Alessandra Totaro, Valerio Venier, Andrea Xompero, Stefano Zen, and Marco Zicari.
Key aspects of this project were the artistic direction of Davide Rampello, who filled the Foundation's new home with life through his dialogue with Venice; the curation of the exhibition space by Orna Cohen and Andreas Heinecke, social entrepreneurs devoted to inclusion and dialogue on issues of diversity understood as value and richness, in great harmony with The Human Safety Net's vision on human potential; the interior design of Migliore+Servetto, who with their drawings gave shape to what was a dream and a vision, with a simplicity full of bold ambitions and care.
We are also grateful to all the people, from Venice and beyond, who have offered their advice, support, observations, and ideas to make this project the best possible. Special thanks go to Renata Codello and Fondazione Giorgio Cini for their close commitment; to Luca Massimo Barbero, for our impromptu dialogues, and for being an important source of enrichment, ideas, and solutions.
We extend our gratitude to Adele Re Rebaudengo, President of the Venice Gardens Foundation and all its Board of Directors, for her foresight and determination in completing the delicate restoration of the Royal Gardens of Venice, which led to landscape architect Paolo Pejrone's skilful and magnificent intervention.

Photo credits
Diana Bagnoli pp. 4, 10, 115, 144, 157, 158, 163, 165, 166–215, 218–219, 221, 228–232, 234, 243
Alessandra Chemollo pp. 21, 22, 43, 53, 55, 151, 155
Richard Davies p. 44, 57
© David Chipperfield Architects Berlin pp. 60-63
Camilla Glorioso p. 238
Guido Guidi pp. 64–113
Martino Lombezzi / Contrasto 6, 8, 12, 18, 40, 117, 118, 122, 125–127, 130, 133, 134, 138, 148, 153, 216, 223, 237, 244
Ico Migliore - Migliore+Servetto p. 241
Francesco Neri p. 121
Rik Nys p. 47
Andrea Pattaro p. 147
Sarah Quill p. 28
Alberto Torsello p. 129
Ute Zscharnt for David Chipperfield Architects p. 48

Agefotostock / Alamy Stock Photo p. 27
© **Archivio fotografico – Fondazione Musei Civici di Venezia** p. 37
© **Graziano Arici / Bidgeman Images** p. 23
Assicurazioni Generali Historical Archive, photo Massimo Goina p. 38
© 2022 **Foto Scala, Firenze** p. 34
© 2022 **Mary Evans / Scala, Firenze** p. 33
Melvyn Longhurst / Alamy Stock Photo p. 141
©Museo delle storie di Bergamo, Archivio fotografico Sestini, Fondo Pepi Merisio p. 31
© 2022 **Museo National Thyssen-Bornemisza / Scala, Firenze** p. 32
Matthias Scholz / Alamy Stock Photo p. 142
© 2022 **Mark E. Smith / Scala, Firenze** p. 24
Petr Svarc / Alamy Stock Photo p. 26

VENICE LAB.
RETHINKING ST. MARK'S SQUARE

Design and layout
Leftloft

Translation
Contextus-We Translate Art (Flavia Franzel)
Guadalupe Nettel's text has been tranlsated by **Rosalind Horne**

Editing
Karen Tomatis

Cover
photography by **Alessandra Chemollo**
Back cover and endpapers
photography by **Martino Lombezzi / Contrasto**

First Edition
April 2022

ISBN 979-12-5463-045-7
www.marsilioeditori.it

Reproduction, printing and binding
Grafiche Antiga SpA
Crocetta del Montello (TV)

For
Marsilio Editori SpA®
In Venice

Available through ARTBOOK | D.A.P.
75 Broad Street, Suite 630
New York, NY 10004
www.artbook.com